# Newcomers to America

IN THEIR OWN WORDS

# Newcomers to America

## STORIES OF TODAY'S YOUNG IMMIGRANTS

## BY JUDITH E. GREENBERG

**FRANKLIN WATTS**
A Division of Grolier Publishing
New York  London  Hong Kong  Sydney
Danbury, Connecticut

*In memory of my mother, Rosalind Schlossberg,*
*and my grandmother Jennie Blum.*

*J.E.G.*

Photographs copyright ©: UPl/Bettmann: pp. 8, 12, 13; National
Park Service: p. 11; Monkmeyer Press: pp. 19 (Mimi Forsyth), 37
(Hugh Rogers), 50 bottom, 52, 76 (all Paul Conklin), 57, 63 (both
Spencer Grant); Impact Visuals: pp. 21 (Thor Swift), 28 (Rick
Reinhard), 50 top (Kathleen Foster), 94 (Robert Fox), 97 (Rick
Reinhard); Ben Klaffke: pp. 40, 58, 67, 68, 72, 80, 86, 90, 102;
Historical Museum of South Florida: p. 47; New York Convention
& Visitors Bureau: p. 101; AIP Emilio Segrè Visual Archives: p. 122.

Library of Congress Cataloging-in-Publication Data

Greenberg, Judith E.
    Newcomers to America / by Judith E. Greenberg.
        p.    cm. — (:In their own words)
    Includes index.
    Summary: Young immigrants from foreign countries relate
their experiences in the United States.
    ISBN 0-531-11256-X
    1. Minorities—United States—Juvenile literature.
    2. Immigrants—United States—Juvenile literature. 3. United
States—Emigration and immigration—Juvenile literature.
    [1. Minorities. 2. Immigrants. 3. United States—Emigration and
immigration.]
    I. Title. II. Series.
    E184.Al.G85   1996
    304.8'73–dc20                                          95-40519
                                                              CIP
                                                              AC

# Contents

# ONE

# Meeting the Newcomers

IMAGINE that your parents have just told you that you will be leaving your home and traveling to a country where everyone speaks a different language and the customs are very different from those you know. To your dismay, you are also told that you cannot take any of your favorite things with you. You must leave behind your pets, your bike, video games, photo albums, sports trophies, clothes, CDs, and all your friends. This vast and traumatic change did actually happen to the people you will read about in this book. Each of the immigrants who speaks to you through this book left his or her homeland as a teenager and came to America, leaving behind a culture, language, and many friends and relatives. These newcomers also left behind the feeling of belonging, of being surrounded by other similar people, and of knowing who they were.

Poverty and persecution in their homelands and the chance for better economic opportunities in America lead many people to leave their homes, their families and

*The joy of achieving citizenship is demonstrated by a crowd of nearly 10,000 people who participated in a huge naturalization ceremony in the Orange Bowl in Florida in 1984.*

friends, their jobs, and their cultures to make difficult journeys in the hope of finding a better life. America has been a magnet for people from all over the world since the earliest days of our nation. Our culture has been described as a melting pot or a salad bowl, reflecting the many people who make up our population. America is a multicultural land, populated by a rich mix of people that has, through the decades, evolved as immigrants have brought new ideas and new customs to their adopted country.

American society today struggles with the problems that develop from the large numbers of immigrants who are settling throughout the United States. However, this is not a new situation. Immigration records from 1789 to 1820 show that approximately 300,000 immigrants came to America in that time period. Immigration was unrestricted, the country was large, and most people already living here had been immigrants themselves, so few problems were recorded. Then suddenly, in the 1840s and 1850s, new waves of immigrants began reaching these shores. They came for a variety of reasons and suffered a variety of problems after they arrived.

The potato famine in Ireland brought great numbers of poor Irish who arrived exhausted from long journeys in crowded ships. They were too poor to travel any farther and so they settled in the eastern cities where they worked in low-paying, hard jobs in factories, canal-building, railroad construction, and mining. Their living conditions were dreadful, with overcrowding, diseases, and crime making their lives more difficult.

Other immigrants from northeastern Europe also began to reach America in great numbers after 1850. Failed revolutions in Germany left many unsuccessful revolutionary leaders and their followers in great danger of reprisals from the German government. These refugees were often well educated and intellectual, as well as leaders in the business community. They first settled in New York City and in the Baltimore, Maryland, areas but later, large numbers established communities in Milwaukee, St. Louis, and Cincinnati.

The states of Minnesota and North and South Dakota were the destination most often sought by immigrants from Sweden, Norway, and Denmark. These newcomers came for good farmland and only began moving into the cities in the late 1890s. Like the Germans who arrived before them, they tended to keep to themselves.

The Chinese immigrants, as a group, endured very difficult times in America. Assimilation was much harder for them; they not only spoke a different language and practiced different customs, but they were also easily identified as foreign. The Gold Rush drew these immigrants seeking to leave behind the overpopulation, poverty, and famines of their country. They took low-paying jobs, often as cooks, launderers, or servants. Japanese immigrants suffered similar discrimination. Like the Scandinavians, the Japanese came seeking good farmland in America.

When the Italians arrived in the late 1890s, they settled in eastern cities and took jobs as laborers, or they made the long trip to California and settled in rich farming areas. Another new immigrant in this period was the eastern European Jew. Over two million Jews came to America from 1881 to 1914, primarily from Poland and Russia where they had been persecuted economically, politically, and for religious reasons. This is when my family members came to America.

"Why do you always want to know about the bad times?" my grandmother questioned me each time I asked her about the old country and how she had come to America. "Ask me instead about the good times in America," she'd say. I already knew that for Sabina Strauss, a young girl of fifteen in the early 1900s, coming to America was the most important event of her life. She would add that the birth of her first child, my mother, was her second most happy day.

10

*Immigrants in the early nineteenth century
arrive at New York harbor.*

My grandmother came to America with her father
and mother and brother and sisters. The immigration offi-
cial who checked her papers found her name too hard to
spell, so he wrote "Jennie," and she used that name for
the rest of her life. Her family settled in Brooklyn, New
York, among people who spoke their language and
observed the same customs and religious holidays. This
helped ease their transition into American life. Jennie's
father opened a restaurant and she became the waitress

CHINESE • GERMAN • CZECHO-SLOVAKIAN • BRAZIL • SPANISH • JEWISH • SCOTCH • ROUMANIAN • ENGL

*The United States as a melting pot is celebrated in this 1926 photograp*

and thus was unable to attend school. She regretted not getting an education and later went to night school to make up for that loss. Jennie also had to deal with "old world" parents who were very strict and often fearful of their daughter becoming too American in her ways. She stayed very close to the traditions of her parents and later faced the same issue with her own children. There was always a concern that the old culture and language would die out.

This fear of losing oneself in America is not unusual. While working on this book, I was struck over and over again by the similarities among the immigrants and their stories, regardless of where they came from or when they came here. These individuals and families left their homelands to search for better living conditions and most did achieve that goal. Yet, many spoke of all that they had given up and the difficulty and pain of balancing their gains and losses. Still, none chose to return to their homelands.

You will be able to read these stories for yourself through the words of the fourteen people in this book.

TRIAN•SLAVIC • ITALIAN • POLISH • RUSSIAN • TURK • GREEK • IRISH • LITHUNIAN•PORTUGESE

*owing the diverse immigrant population at Public School 1 in New York City.*

Through their interview excerpts, you can understand what it is like to say farewell to all that is familiar and to cross waterways or continents to make a fresh start in America. The people in this book are real immigrants, who tell their stories and describe their feelings about their experiences—some for the very first time. All but one, Yetta, were interviewed specifically for this book. Shortly before she died, Yetta was interviewed by her grand-daughter on the occasion of the birth of her great-grand-daughter. That videotape was made available to me, and I have chosen several excerpts to represent the time peri-od of the early 1900s and thus allow the reader to make comparisons with the more modern immigrants in this book. The hopes and troubles that drove the earlier European and Asian immigrants here still resonate in the words of today's waves of newcomers. Each individual and his or her story is unique, yet many common threads appear throughout the interviews, and the speakers often echo each other's concerns.

There have been many studies of the patterns, or waves, of immigration and the effects of these newcomers on the economy and political system of the United States. News articles about immigration appear in newspapers on an everyday or weekly basis. One only need look in on a typical classroom in America to see a reflection of the makeup of this generation of immigrants. It is important to remember that even today, whether their ancestors came by choice or were forced here, every American is either an immigrant or the descendant of immigrants. Even the earliest inhabitants of this land, Native Americans, are descended from people who crossed the land bridge from Siberia to this continent thousands of years ago. It is really the voices and experiences of all these Americans that have shaped our country and our lives today.

I have attempted to include in this survey of the new generation of immigrants representatives of many of the ethnic or religious groups who have found new homes and lives in America today. I have focused on people who were teenagers or very close to their teen years when they arrived, and who represent countries from which large numbers of immigrants came to America in the second half of the twentieth century. The early twentieth century interview (with Yetta), as well as those from the 1950s era, are included to help the reader compare the immigrants' experiences and to better understand some of the historical waves of immigration to America.

I struggled to select a fair sample of people from various geographic and cultural areas of the world. If space allowed, every ethnic group that has immigrated in large numbers to America would be represented. However, space, and the reluctance of some people to talk about their experiences were the two main limiting factors, and this explains why some immigrant or ethnic groups do not appear in this book. The reader will probably notice that more women than men have been interviewed for this book. This is due to the greater willingness of many women to participate. Some of the interviewees wished to remain anonymous and their names have been changed. Most wanted only a first name used, and I have abided by all their wishes.

Now I would like to introduce each newcomer to you. These are the people you will meet:

**Yetta** came to America in the early part of the twentieth century, when she was thirteen years old. A relative in the United States sent a ticket for her when she was only nine, but her parents didn't want her to leave at such a young age and hid the ticket until she was older. She came by ship as a second-class passenger and had an easier trip than many Europeans of the time who came third class or "steerage class" and spent most of their voyage in the cargo-like hold of the ship.

**Miki** left a home not once, but twice. After a childhood in what was Czechoslovakia, she lived in Israel. Unhappy about the uprooting on both occasions, her words point out the wrenching feelings of her move to America in the 1950s. She also tells about how American teens sometimes treat people who appear to be different.

**Maureen,** leaving behind a family in Ireland that was experiencing some difficulty, also came to America in the 1950s. She traveled a very difficult journey by herself, reaching her new country and new life to live with an aunt and uncle and attend school in a land very different from her homeland.

**Chandler** is the proud owner of the Cafe Xpress in the Washington, D.C., metropolitan area. He left India as a teenager in the mid-1970s when his father was offered a job here and brought the whole family with him. Chandler now employs new immigrants in his business to help them get a start in this country.

**Ann** is a soft-spoken, lovely young woman who left Vietnam to escape life under communist rule. Her parents, of Chinese descent, were immigrants to

Vietnam and experienced discrimination in that country. Ann grew up feeling Vietnamese as well as Chinese. Later, the whole family came to America and today she lives with them and works two jobs in the hope of saving enough money to help support the family and to one day return to college.

**Enrique** is a poet and actor who also works with Latino youths. In 1980, at age fifteen, he escaped from his country, El Salvador, and came to the United States. Guerilla fighting was escalating and his mother, who was already in America, helped to bring him out safely. His culture shock on arriving in America was quite unlike that of any of the other immigrants who speak in this book.

**Carlos** left Mexico with his family when he was fifteen years old, in the 1980s, and arrived in California. Today he works for a Latin American social services agency. He is one of the immigrants who first described to me the feeling of always being a foreigner in this country.

**Nilou** escaped from Iran in 1985 when she was an elementary school student. She is now a senior in high school. Although she felt her escape from Iran was an exciting adventure, the dangers were very real. Her family—including her mother who was pregnant at the time—left most of their belongings behind and had to travel for months while they waited for visas to enter the United States.

**Gabi** came to her new home—with her family and her dog—from Lithuania in the 1980s. Her experience as a young teenager shows how difficult such a move can be. Gabi's story is particularly moving as her homeland is now independent after the breakup of the Soviet Union.

**Fassil** and his brother came to America in the 1980s from Africa so that they could go to college. Fassil now works for a law firm and makes his home in the United States. He rarely returns to his native land.

**Erika** is from Ecuador, the country she left in 1985, just one day before her sixteenth birthday. With her were her mother and a sister and brother. She had to learn how to survive in a hurry when she arrived as she was the new kid in school. Today she has her own business and works hard to make it a success.

**Anna** is currently the president of the International Student Club on the campus of Morgan State University in Baltimore, Maryland. She has been in America only a few years after escaping from her country of Liberia during its Civil War.

**Alice** came here from the Caribbean island of Nevis when she was a teen. She has a job in an office now and is bright and hardworking. She has recently gained a sense of a new pride in her heritage.

**Soo** is now a minister in a Korean church where he works with the young people of his congregation. Like Soo, many of the congregants are new to America and his experiences as an immigrant from Korea help him to relate to their special needs and hopes.

As you read this book, try to picture each interviewee as a unique person and think about the forces that have shaped his or her life. Draw your own conclusions about the modern immigrant experience, and use this information to help you appreciate and understand the complex culture that is America today and how you play a role as a citizen of this multicultural society.

# TWO

# Coming to America

AMERICA has always been known as a nation of nations. The difference now is that the newcomers are not primarily from Europe, as was the case with our earlier waves of immigration, but from other areas of the world. Europeans make up only 10 percent of today's immigrants as opposed to 85 percent at the turn of the century, when Yetta came here. This difference may be one of the reasons why state and federal governments, school systems, and communities are so worried about the current wave of immigrants. It seems easier to absorb European immigrants as so many of today's Americans are descended from European ancestry. However, the bulk of immigrants since 1970 have been from Japan, Korea, Eastern Europe, China and Taiwan, the Philippines, the mid-eastern countries, Vietnam, Mexico, Cuba, and other Latino countries. Nearly every country on the face of our planet has some people now living in the United States. The question becomes, can we

*Today's immigrants arrive from many
different countries of the world.*

as a society continue to absorb these masses of people of different backgrounds?

Studies of immigrants who came here from Asian and Hispanic nations from 1970 on, show that these people are following the same patterns the earlier immigrants did. After an initial period of adjustment and struggle, they are now moving into the suburbs, furthering their children's educations, buying homes, and developing middle-class status. Looking at the past ten or fifteen years,

19

researchers agree that the immigrants are adapting to and succeeding in the American culture. They are working and paying taxes and helping our economy. These facts should show that the fears of Americans who worried that today's immigrants would not assimilate are not valid. Unfortunately, these studies do not take into account illegal immigrants, whose numbers, by some accounts, may be as large as those of the legal newcomers.

If current immigration and birth rates continue to grow, our American society will look quite different in the near future. It is estimated that by the year 2025, the population of school age Americans will be about equally divided between whites and people of color. Community leaders should begin to take stock of their plans and realize that no ethnic group will have a majority. Very soon the black and Hispanic populations will be equal in size and often competing for the same social services.

One concern of local and state governments in this country is that the immigrant population is not distributed equally throughout the country. Although immigrants have settled in virtually every state, several states have been inundated with large populations of legal and illegal immigrants. This has caused financial and sometimes social service problems for those states. For example, in 1990, 1.5 billion immigrants arrived in America. Nearly 80 percent of them settled in California, Florida, Texas, New York, New Jersey, and Illinois. Washington, D.C., has also been the destination of many newcomers. However, California has taken the most, with 44 percent of the immigrants heading there.

With the passage of Proposition 187 in California, immigration has become a topic of concern in the newspapers and on TV weekly, if not daily. On November 8, 1994, California voters approved Proposition 187 by a 59–41 percent margin. The proposition is designed to broadly deny public education, nonemergency health services, and other social services to illegal immigrants.

*In California, in 1994, student groups organized marches to protest the passage of Proposition 187, which would cut off public education and all but emergency medical services to illegal immigrants and their children.*

Analysts for the state of California estimate that reducing these services would save approximately 200 million dollars a year. The restrictions on health services were to become effective on January 1, 1996; however a federal court has barred the implementation and also blocked the restrictions on education.

One obstacle to Proposition 187 is the 1982 Supreme Court decision in *Plyer v. Doe,* which found that states could not deny equal access to public elementary and secondary schools to illegal aliens. But supporters of the proposition say that educating the children of illegal immigrants costs the state nearly 1.6 billion dollars, as 40 percent of the 3.2 million illegals live in California. Opponents of the proposition point out that the illegal children count in the state's total number of school children and eliminating them would greatly reduce the federal funds received by the state. Further, those students would then face enormous obstacles in achieving assimilation into American society.

School officials are caught in the dilemma. "What do I do when the children come to school? I can't push them away," asks a school principal in Los Angeles. Many superintendents and principals in California are themselves immigrants from Cuba or other Latino countries and these men and women know that the mix of cultures and experiences enriches the classroom.

Some critics of immigration say that even legal immigrants come here only to use our social services and get an education. I did not find this to be true. The sample of people I interviewed and the studies I've read show that immigrants come here to reunite with family members, to find employment, and to get a chance to build a better life. These are the same reasons most of our grandparents and great-grandparents have come here since this nation of nations was founded in the 1770s.

---

## THE IMMIGRANTS REMEMBER

— Where are you originally from and how old were you when you came to America?
— What family members accompanied you on the journey?
— What do you remember about why you left and the preparations for leaving?

— How did you feel about coming to America?
— Where did you first arrive in the United States
and how was it decided where you would live?

**Yetta**

I was thirteen years old when I came to America on
August 13, 1913. I got a boat ticket from my cousin who
sent it over for me, and my family in Europe had it for
four years before they told me. The ticket came in 1909
and they kept it because they didn't want me to go to
America. Nobody wanted me to go but I found out
about the ticket because my cousins in America sent a
telegram. I started to insist that I wanted to go, and my
parents finally gave me permission to go for a few
months; but then I would have to come back to Poland.
When the few months were up, the First World War
broke out so I couldn't go back and I was thankful that I
remained in America.

I had thirteen brothers and sisters. Six died as infants
so, all together we were five brothers and two sisters who
grew up. In Poland, we had a big apartment with six
rooms in a nice red brick building. I shared a room with
my sister. We were always running and fighting, fighting
as a joke. We had a big dining room with a table that we
would run all around, my older sister and me. She was
two years older; I was the youngest. I missed her when I
left; Hitler got her. Hitler got her and my brother Solomon
and his two daughters, and my sister and her son and
daughter and the whole big family were burned. [Yetta is
referring to World War II and the Nazi regime.]

When I first came here I went to Hoboken [New
Jersey]. I came on a second-class ticket so I didn't go
through Ellis Island. We came straight off the boat because only third-class passengers went through Ellis
Island. Then, on my first Friday night, my brother took

me to a cousin's house for dinner. We had dinner and then my brother said, "Yetta, come home." And I said "Are you crazy? Today is Friday, we are not going to ride." But he wanted me to come home. He said we had to go, and I was afraid that we would fall down and die for traveling on a Friday night. [Yetta had been brought up as an Orthodox Jew and she had never ridden on the Sabbath.]

## Miki

I was born in France, I grew up in what was then Czechoslovakia and then lived in Israel. I was sixteen when I came here from Israel with my parents and sister. It was 1955.

You ask me why my family left Israel—I think it was a combination of factors. The most important one, at least for my parents, was that they really did not want us to go into the Israeli army, which we would have had to do, had we stayed. The other reason was that it was always my father's dream to come to the United States. When he was growing up in Czechoslovakia, he had an uncle who lived in the United States and was one of the owners of a big shipping company that had a cruise ship. Every so often he would come to visit his family in Czechoslovakia and bring toys, so as a young kid, my father already had this image of America as a place he wanted to go. Before World War II he had papers to go to the United States, but when the war broke out, he couldn't, so I think he carried the dream with him. Then after spending the war years in England, my father went back to Czechoslovakia to see if anybody had survived. He found that nobody had. He stayed and I was born. But then the communists came. We escaped the communists and went to Israel. Just a couple of days after we left, the communists took over.

We left in a big hurry, we barely took anything, and even the few things that we packed were not there when we got to Israel. For instance, my dad wanted to take his good camera because he thought that he could use it. He had a very sophisticated camera, but when we got to Israel in 1950, there were rags in the suitcase and no camera.

I have very few memories of leaving except that I had a terrible fear of flying. I developed a fever, a very high fever, so we didn't go the day that we were supposed to go and the plane we were supposed to be on was shot down over Bulgaria. I guess my illness saved our lives.

## Maureen

I'm from Dublin, the capital in Ireland, and I was thirteen when I came here. In 1955 I came by myself to live with an aunt, my mother's half sister, who lived in Rochester, New York. I came by boat, it was a freighter, and it took nineteen days. It was a very small boat and we ran into storms. Imagine people coming by boat in the fifties—it was almost like the days when Irish people came in the ship's hold, but it was actually very service-oriented. They took on five passengers, I suppose for extra income, so we sat with the captain in his dining room, the food was very elegant and the service beautiful.

Because I was a child I wasn't scared, but, I think for the adults it might have been scary because it was a tiny boat and we ran into storms. It didn't bother me at all except I got sick, but it was probably frightening to some people. To me, it was an adventure. I didn't realize how serious the situation was.

I come from kind of a comfortable upper middle-class family. The reasons I came had a lot to do with my father, who was in poor health. I guess it started in the 1940s. He was working at night and he had a favorite friend from Hungary who told him about a wonder drug that would keep him awake at night. It was very helpful to him. He was functioning in his job under a lot of strain during the war [World War II] and I'm not making excuses for him, because I knew other people didn't become addicted to drugs, but to make a long story short, he became addicted and lost his job and was unable to support our family.

My mother felt it was upsetting me very much. I was the favorite and I think there were many factors that influenced my leaving. I think mother said to father, "now see what you've done, you've ruined our family. You are losing your only daughter because we can't afford to keep going and my sister has invited her to live there [in the United States] for a year."

The other factor was that in Ireland secondary school at that time was not free. My brother was considered brilliant. I was considered very bright too, but, before my aunt died, she told me that the real reason she sent for me was to see that my brother was the one who would get the chance for school in Ireland. However, I take that with a grain of salt. I feel it was a combination of complex issues, economics, and a little bit psychological, and also my father's inability to support our family and get control of himself, which he did years later, but by then I was here.

I don't know how relevant this is, well, I don't think it is typical, but I left a very happy life in Ireland, believe it or not. I was happy in spite of my father's problems, with lots of friends. Then I was on the ocean. It was beautiful in Ireland, and everything was lovely except for the thing that was going on with my father. My aunt was a very bitter woman. Since my mother didn't have the money to come to America and drag me back after being here in school for one year, one year led to another, and by the time I realized it I was finished with high school. At that point, I wanted to go to college so I stayed on my own for three more years. I guess many immigrant stories are like that.

I was a little apprehensive [about going to America] but I thought it would be an exciting adventure, and since it was only supposed to last for a year, so, okay, it wouldn't be that terrible. I thought it was weird, very weird, I felt almost as if I was on another planet. I landed in Philadelphia in the middle of the night and I couldn't figure out what some buildings were. It turned out that

Philadelphia, at that time, still had a lot of refineries and natural gas plants and factories. I waited all night in the terminal. Then my aunt arrived in the morning and at first we talked but we had a two-hour wait for a bus and this weird music was playing from a jukebox, all these awful songs of Elvis Presley and Johnny Ray. I think one was that awful song "Cry." Some people love those singers but I'm very opinionated. Anyway, for two hours we listened to this weird music over and over again and I just couldn't get over it. We stopped talking and then, on the bus coming to Rochester, we got along wonderfully. You know, I was shocked by the weather, too, because it was so cold and there was snow. Then in a few days, I started high school.

## Chandler

Hi, my name is Chandler. In 1975, I had just turned thirteen and I came to America from India. My father got a job offer so we moved.

My brother and I thought it would be good to move, but my mom had mixed feelings. She did not want to leave the country because I had an older brother and sister there. She didn't want to leave them and after you live in one place for so many years you don't want to leave your family and friends. We had a house there, and my oldest brother was living in it, too, so, we left everything other than our clothes and left the house the way it was, and it is still there.

My father was working in Washington, D.C., and when we first came we stayed at the Ritz Carlton Hotel. We stayed there about fifteen months and then we moved to suburban Maryland.

## Ann

I was twelve years old when I came here with my family, which included my seven brothers and sisters. We came to Philadelphia in the late 1970s. We stayed for a week

and my mom did not like Philadelphia because the place was too quiet. She wanted to move to Washington because my second brother who came to this country six months before we did was there. My parents wanted to be close to my brother so we decided to move to Washington, D.C. Why did we want to leave Vietnam? Because of the communists, that's why we had to leave there.

My parents decided to go because when we were in Vietnam and the communists came, we lost our business. We had no business left so we could not make money. That is why we had to leave our country to come here. Before we left, a couple of months or six months before, my mother prepared everything. My father paid someone who knew how to escape from Vietnam to another country. We had to pay for each person to escape from Vietnam. Each person cost—how much? My mother told me, I forgot—a lot of money for each country we went through. I know it cost a lot for each person to come here but we came. We left Vietnam in 1978, came to Hong Kong, stayed there for a year, and then we came here in 1980. The house that we lived in in Vietnam didn't belong to us; it belonged to the government. We just rented and slept there, so you know we left everything. We left the property and took everything we have, which was clothes. My grandparents died a long time ago, so nobody was left there. I had seven brothers and sisters, including me eight, so everybody left there—no family members at all stayed behind.

Of course, I feel I miss my friends, my neighborhood there. But I was small and I didn't feel it like my mother

*The goal for most immigrants is citizenship—with all the rights and the obligations this status includes.*

did. It was okay for me, you know. My mother said she
wanted to leave the country, and we just go wherever she
wants to go. I just follow my family. I didn't know any
English before I left, not even ABC or 12345, none at all.

## Enrique
My mother had been here since 1969. I came from war-
torn El Salvador in 1980, when I was fifteen, to live with
my family that was already here. It was planned for us all
to come here. Mom left in 1969, then we were supposed
to come one by one. There were five of us, and I was the
third one who was supposed to come here but because in
1980 a lot was going on in my life that could have made it
difficult for me to stay longer—the political situation, the
war, the guerillas—I had a choice of either joining the
guerillas, against my government, or leaving. Relatives
took me to get my visa at the American Embassy. But I
couldn't get a visa right away and I was told I was on the
hit list of the National Guard. The mayor of the town
came to me and said, "You are on the list so you better
get the hell out of here and go somewhere else." So I left,
and that's the way it happened.

I had approximately two weeks to escape. The morning I left town there were already a lot of refugees, and
fighting going on all around. I spent a couple of days on
the road and got to the next town, about thirty miles
away, and then I flew to D.C.

I had sort of known, since my mom left, that the plan
was that I would come here and we would be together as
a family, because my mom had worked very hard and
made opportunities for me. But, at that time, I really did-
n't want to come. I had a lot of things I was involved in
and I really believed in the war. Actually, I tried to join
another guerilla movement. I had planned to escape or
run away with the family to another camp, and it was not
my wish to come here at that time, you know. I was com-
mitted to other things. I hated it when I first came.

## Carlos

My name is Juan Carlos. I am from Mexico City in Mexico and I was thirteen when I came with my family to California. My mom was already in the United States and she came to get us. We had a very sudden leave-taking. She was there for about a month and we had some time to prepare but it still felt very sudden to me. I also felt very sad about coming to America because I had to leave my friends and my grandparents behind. I did not speak any English before I came.

## Nilou

I was eight years old when I first came. I had lived in Iran and I came with my mother and father in 1985. My brothers came a year before us; they were, I think, fourteen and fifteen when they came. They came with other friends about their age, and then they met my aunt here.

We are Jewish, a minority in Iran and minorities are usually picked on. It was a bad situation. Where the schools were integrated with Jewish and non-Jewish students, they made us attend on Saturdays [the Sabbath] and stuff like that. We didn't have as many freedoms as the other people. Well, to leave, we had to sell all of our things. Everything had to be hush-hush. Everything had to be done very carefully because if we were found out, if the government found out, we'd be executed. So we had to sell all of our stuff.

My parents told us that we were leaving because of the army. Once in awhile, the government's people would go through the streets and pick up anybody who was physically old enough [to serve in the army]. They were not given the proper training that they give in other countries. Yeah, it was really, really dangerous and most people didn't come back from the army. My mother felt she had to leave; she did not want to send my brothers to America alone. We went to New York City. My cousins met us at JFK airport, and we stayed with them for awhile and then we went to New Orleans and then Maryland. It was hard; I didn't speak any English.

## Gabi

In 1989, I was one month away from turning thirteen, when I came with my parents from Lithuania. We came by plane, and we came right to Washington—me, my parents and my dog. My father's family is here and my father wanted to come—he thought it would be better for him and his family. His whole family is here. The economic situation was getting pretty bad in Lithuania and my father thought it would be good for us to be here. I didn't want to come and I guess it felt like I was losing all my friends and pretty much everything I ever knew.

## Fassil

I come from Ethiopia, that is in Africa, I was nineteen when I first came here in the 1980s. I came with my older brother who is a year and four months older. First, we came to Missouri. We landed in Chicago, then we flew on to Missouri. I had just finished high school. I came to America to go to school here, three years of college that's why I came.

I was very happy about coming here, but our parents were the ones who were excited that we were going overseas to study. Father wanted me to be a law student and he said we should go over after high school and study.

## Erika

When I first came here from Ecuador, I came with my mom and my little brother. Do you want me to tell you why I came? Well, it is not easy to say why I came here. When I was in Ecuador my parents had problems between them, and one day my mom decided to come here and took my brother and me. She talked about it with my older sister, my brother, and me, but she didn't tell my dad, because, you know, of the problems that some people have in marriage. In Ecuador women like my mother did not have to work or worry about food or anything. We used to study and stay home and my mom too. In America it is different. I'm working here; I just have to work. And it was not easy because we did not know how to speak English. We didn't know how. We had come here before but just for vacations. We didn't know hardly anyone in the United States. So . . . a big change. I just have my aunt here and one uncle. I came here just one day before I was going to be sixteen.

## Anna

I was seventeen when I fled Liberia with my whole family in the late 1980s. There was a civil war in my country and it was getting worse and worse. The rebels were bombing nearby and schools were closing to keep the children home where they might be safer. The rebels and the fighting were getting closer to my city and the fighting was very heavy. My parents had talked about our leaving before, but now they decided it must be immediate. We had little time to prepare; we left in a hurry, and left most of our things behind. We got out by plane only shortly before the airports were closed. We found out later that our home was bombed just one week after we had left.

We came to New York City and I stayed for three months with an aunt and uncle. Then I moved to Baltimore to be with another aunt.

## Alice

I was ten when I came with my mother and one sister and two brothers. My dad, he was the reason we came. He was born in Nevis and came over at a very young age. His family migrated here with my grandmother and he went to school, law school, and the whole bit. Then he couldn't find a job because of racism. His mom told him, "Why don't you go home and take a vacation?" So he met my mom, they married, and he decided to set up his own practice in Nevis—but he died. He had cancer and he died in 1964. After that time my mom left the four younger children in Nevis and she decided to come up to the States because her mom had already been here for years and so was my father's mom, so she brought us here.

We came up in April; there was a big snow and we came into New York. That's where my grandmother lived at the time and I couldn't stand it; I was absolutely frozen. I was cold; I didn't like it. It was spring, but it was very cold, and I fought for months actually because I wanted to go back to the Islands.

## Soo

I'm from Korea. I left at six years old. In 1965, we stopped at Norway and then went on to South America. We were there for seven years until 1972. When I was thirteen, we moved to the United States, and lived in Chicago for three years. Basically, we left for business reasons. Well, we had to sell our house and leave a lot behind, but we took a lot with us. We went by ship in 1965. It took us two months to get to South America, a wonderful trip.

When we arrived in Paraguay it was a new land, culture, and language. We didn't know anybody. My first year of school there was very traumatic. I was only six years old. I was in a Spanish-speaking school. Eventually and basically for educational reasons, since by that time my older brother was eighteen, we decided to come to the United States.

When we knew we were going to move to the United States, my parents put us—the children—in an English class for six months. Also, we went to an international school where there were a lot of foreigners. There were some Embassy children so we had contact with other people who didn't necessarily speak English well. The trip to the United States was not difficult.

# THREE

# First Impressions of America and My Neighborhood

THE PICTURE of America most immigrants have in mind is one that rarely shows slums, pollution, or poverty. Newcomers come hoping to achieve a piece of the American dream. If not, why would they come? For large numbers of immigrants, hard work, education, and time allow them to realize their dreams. But for many, the initial experience of life in the United States is very far from the images they brought with them.

Of the 250 million Americans, 20 percent are African-American, Native American, or Asian-American. Another 9 percent are Hispanic-American. Thirty-two million people in the United States speak a language other than English at home. In California alone, 5.5 million people speak Spanish and over one-half million speak Chinese at home. In all, over 17 million people living in the United States speak Spanish at home. Many of these people are newcomers to the United States.

Immigrants are frequently forced, by economic necessity, to live in low-income communities. These communities are often near hazardous waste sites that can affect the health and safety of the inhabitants. The United States Environmental Protection Agency created the Office of Environmental Justice in 1992, to address the environmental impact on these minority and newcomer communities.

The Office of Environmental Justice seeks to ensure that all people, regardless of ethnicity or income, have an opportunity to live in a healthy environment. They should have clean air to breathe, clean water to drink, and uncontaminated foods to eat. Unfortunately, many immigrants live in polluted and less desirable areas. For some, this is not a change from their homelands, but for others, it is a frightening experience.

Before coming to America, immigrants often have a "Hollywood" or movie screen concept of this country. Living with environmental hazards is not part of the picture in their heads. Many of the newcomers who were interviewed talked about the old movies that had shaped their image of America, and then—once they arrived— the harsh and strange reality that greeted them.

Low-income workers are more likely to live near landfills, incinerators, and hazardous waste treatment facilities. Of course, these waste sites are found in middle-class and even wealthy communities, but not in the numbers of those in poorer areas. In many cases, the hazardous site has been there for many decades, perhaps from an old silver mine or lumber treatment plant. Low-income housing has been built up around it and now the newcomers

*Immigrant families often find the only affordable housing is in the shadow of environmental hazards.*

live with the problem. Children are especially vulnerable to harm from toxic substances.

People living in poverty and people of color cannot always move away from these environmental problems. Of those newcomers interviewed for this book, several started out in such communities. Now they all feel that their hard work and determination to better themselves through education as well as working together has helped them move to safer communities.

## THE IMMIGRANTS REMEMBER
— **What did you think America would be like?**
— **What was your first impression of America when you actually got here?**
— **Did you want to go back home?**
— **How were you treated by the Americans you met?**

### Miki
I was invited to dinner by a typical American family because they wanted to introduce me to Thanksgiving and let me feel how a real Thanksgiving feast feels. They were very nice and always respectful and warm. My sister ended up making many friends—because she was younger, it was easier. I think that a couple of years after we came people still thought we were foreigners.

### Maureen
They [the kids at school] tried to be nice to me, some of them tried to be, and I might have been a little standoffish. That could have been a lot of the reason why I didn't feel welcome. I thought the language would be easy but it wasn't. I thought I was to be a companion to my younger cousin, but that didn't work out either.

I thought the music was so strange and the people

kept missing the little things that mattered. I felt pushed into changing or I would be alone and feel like Cinderella.

## Chandler

My first impression of the United States? I thought living in D.C. was going to be terrific, and that this part of America was very neat and clean. I had a different picture of it, you know, the impression in my head. D.C. is good, but in some places there are a lot of buildings, and some streets of the area are not a pretty sight. After awhile we moved to Maryland and Virginia and since then, I kind of like it.

I didn't want to go home right away, not really. I liked that America was different, and everything was easy. To get to the stores, you go one place and shop for everything instead of stopping in four or five. In India, usually, you stop in four or five different places if you want to buy groceries. Here, you make just one stop, so that's kind of neat.

I understood everything, but sometimes some words were different. In our country some words are like English, because the British ruled India for many years. One day we went into the store with my father and my father wanted to buy a vegetable, okra, but he called okra, lady finger. We were in a small store downtown and my father kept on looking at the board to find the okra. My dad kept saying "we call them lady fingers in India and I don't see it on the board." But there were some right behind him. It was real funny, but it was finally okay. We got what we needed.

## Ann

When I first moved to the United States, I felt like it was boring. The place that we lived was too quiet, not many people around us, we always had to stay at home—so boring, so different from my country. In Vietnam, my country, so many people are in the house, in the street, outside,

*An immigrant family living in public housing*

and we talk a lot and we have fun playing. Here it is so different, so I feel it's boring, that's all. Today, in Vietnam a lot is going on, a lot of activity going on, always.

At first, I felt like I wanted to go right home, but now I don't have that feeling anymore. The Americans are pretty fair, so far. There are nice American people with no problem with immigrants. I think they are very kind and nice to new people.

We really didn't know what America would be like, we didn't think about that, we knew it had to be better than what was in Vietnam then. We were so nervous when we left, we were just happy we were still alive. We came on a big ship with more than 3,000 people, a big ship. We didn't know if we would still be alive at the end of the trip. My parents were so scared. We were lucky we got out of there, with everybody saved, you know, nobody any problem.

## Enrique

For me, television showed America. I expected to come to a young country basically, with a lot of material things, but other than language, not much different from my land. The American music and movies I had watched pretty much showed life in a glossy America. My image of America was of clean, neat houses and happy people.

And then I came to D.C. and lived in a mostly poor neighborhood, where poor blacks and Latinos lived. This was reality and not like in the movies. We were always treated as someone of color. My misconceptions caused a lot of confusion in my life. I had watched a TV special about where I thought we would live and then we got here and reality was pretty much of a shock.

## Carlos

I thought living in America was going to be wonderful. I thought that it would be very luxurious because of the movies and because of the things that my mom had said in her letters—things that other people had said too.

When I first came to America it was not what I thought it would be. I did think it was wonderful and everything, physically, but it was sad because I felt like we were always working. I thought it was so different from my life in Mexico where our lives were not so focused on our careers and more on being with our families. I grew up in a big city so it wasn't just a change from small town to big city but such a change in the priorities of the people.

Television influenced a lot of my behavior and the things I thought. I thought they [people on television] were real and I tried to imitate them a lot. I ended up in a kind of la-la land, you know. As I grew older I realized that that's not real and I tried to find my way in the new place I had to adjust to.

## Nilou

I liked it, I thought coming to America would be so futuristic. The ecology would be far ahead of my old country and things would be so exciting and strange. What makes a difference to a child about living in some countries? I thought it would all be Disneyland. Looking at the pictures of America, I never thought anything bad. I never knew about pollution or anything. But when I got here, my first impression wasn't Disneyland. No, it wasn't, it was hard here because I did not know any English. My cousins did and it was really hard because I couldn't handle it. No one was really my age, my brothers were older, and my cousins were younger, and it wasn't so much fun at all. We were with them for about six months. Then we came to Maryland and I think I felt better about how America looked. Maybe because we were just our family.

I was left on my own, they [American students] didn't bother with me, they really stayed away from me. It took me a long time to catch on to how to act and deal with Americans.

## Gabi

My first impression of America, I remember feeling that people viewed me as different, always staring; everything was a change for me. We lived in the capital in Lithuania so it wasn't just a change from small town to big city. It was a great change altogether.

The way it all looked, the people, everything was different. Oh, back then, yeah I was quite unhappy for awhile, I thought it would be better to go home. I had two cousins, they were four and seven years older than me, who had come here five years before we did. They did help since they were here earlier, and it helped me a lot, but it wasn't like a very close relationship.

## Fassil

I had never been in the United States before. The first impression was probably the buildings, that is what impressed me the most. Then when we landed in Chicago, the size of the city and the mountains we could see. The city and the mountains and the roads—I would never think there were so many highways and freeways. Then, we lived in Missouri. I saw many different parts of what I thought was America.

I was treated fairly [by Americans], and there was no language problem. My brother and I spoke English before we came. I really honestly cannot say I had problems when I got here because I had gone to an American school, a Catholic school that was run by Americans back home. I did have an opinion as to what America and Americans would be like, and it really wasn't that different at all.

## Erika

Well, what did I first think when I got here from Equador? I came here to live in Maryland. I have to say this country is so beautiful; it has many things. This is bigger than my country; my country is little. My people care about you, so when I came here, I was surprised nobody cared about me. I didn't know anybody here. It was difficult to stay. I didn't have to work in my country, so when I came here I had to take care of my brother because my mother was working. It was a new thing for me. It was a very big change.

But, American people are good, I guess, because they came here like us. They came here from other countries. And that is what this is all about; this country was made by immigrants. They're good because they want to give their hope to other people.

I tried to know about America by watching movies and matching the action with the words. You don't understand at first, but when you watch the movie twice or three times you finally understand. You try to know what the meaning is. But what is on TV is not always what the people are like. Sometimes they are better and sometimes not. Sometimes the place to live for newcomers is not so good either.

## Anna

I was terrified! New York and then Baltimore scared me half to death. I was seventeen but I cried nearly every night. All around me, it seemed, were drugs and people being shot, and a very scary way of living. I was not prepared for this, my hometown in Liberia was so sheltered by comparison and I was in constant fear of the night.

## Alice

No, the English language was not a factor for me. My impressions—well it was just the whole thing. I think the United States was so huge, New York City was so large with all the neighbors and all the people running around, all the cars, all the dark and dirty looking places; I think it was overwhelming for me. I think about the atmosphere in the islands, my home in Nevis, a big yard, one or two cars around. To me the city was so very different.

It was very traumatic and I think it has affected my entire life. This is the first time I have looked back on it and thought about the things that happened through my life. What I am going through now as an adult is a result of that experience.

## Soo

We thought we knew what it was like in America. When we got here and were living in Chicago, we had a pastor who constantly talked to us. We also met someone from South America who had moved to the United States before us and they pretty well showed us around and gave us introductions to the culture, basically taught us how to use the system, helped us find an apartment, and so forth.

At home, the movies and everything we saw showed Americans. That gave us an idea of the houses that they had, what people would be like, and so forth.

At first, America reminded me of home, lots of grass, enough for everyone, typical happy days, houses and neighborhoods. But then I saw different kinds of neighborhoods from those I had seen on television. There were row houses and apartment complexes. I wasn't so much disappointed, it was just different.

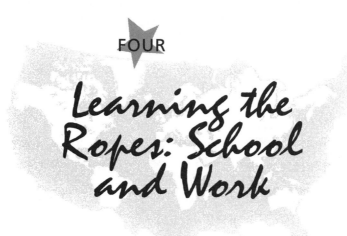

# FOUR

# Learning the Ropes: School and Work

THE FIRST DAY of school, and other particular school days, always stay in our memories. We can recall individual events, both good and bad and remember how we felt on eventful days. Perhaps we worried about getting the combination right on the locker, or getting from one class at the end of the hall to the next class downstairs and across the school building. Maybe changing clothes in gym class was a horror for some. But all of these, as painful as they may be, do not compare to the fear and often pain that immigrant teenagers face as they walk through the doors of an American school for the first time. Sadly, our schools are not set up to handle the needs of the immigrants. While they offer many helpful programs including Limited English Proficiency classes and international clubs, the biggest problem seems to be that Americans are impatient with people who do not immediately understand what exactly is expected of them. Even simple things like going to the lunchroom or turning in homework assignments can be confusing and fright-

*In recent years, political turmoil in Haiti, Vietnam,
Cuba, and elsewhere has resulted in boatloads of
refugees coming to American shores.*

ening. A teen immigrant's transition into the community
of an American school is often shaped by the reasons why
he or she left the homeland, who came with them, and
what the trip was like. A successful transition also depends
on the coping skills of the immigrant.

The circumstances of why a family leaves a homeland
and how they get here actually affects their getting started in America. When immigrants arrive in the United
States, they have experienced many traumas such as ill-

ness, sleeping in fields, facing hostile border guards or angry soldiers along their route. For those immigrants who are also refugees, there are psychological factors that compound their problems. While trying to learn how to survive in a new country, the immigrant must also deal with tragic losses, such as family members who were left behind, or professional careers that are lost, and most especially the sense of belonging to a nation that they can call their own. They have left their friends, familiar surroundings, and a sense of where and how things work. In exchange they are now bewildered, overworked, and often the victims of new types of discrimination.

Every immigrant must develop survival skills to get through this difficult adjustment period. The immigrants in this book often mentioned the need to work hard, and to persevere through the feelings of isolation and bewilderment that they often felt in the first few years in America. These are important skills, yet one should also add the ability to bend on the outside in those circumstances that are beyond a person's control. At the same time, keeping a sense of self-worth on the inside is definitely necessary. It is vital for immigrants to set goals and then adjust their behavior to face the numerous changes and challenges that come along. Those who do overcome the obstacles often feel they have had to suppress their emotions during this time and that it is hard to bring the emotions back once they feel safe and have grown up. Most of the teen interviewees stated that their self-esteem was greatly affected by language difficulties, cultural differences, and the sense of not knowing what to do in many school or public situations. The immigrants felt isolated and lost in their new country.

For those immigrants who come to America as refugees, their sense of isolation is compounded by the experiences preceding their arrival. Many, like Nilou, Anna, and Enrique, barely escaped with their lives. Others actually suffered imprisonment, death of family members, loss of home and possessions, repeated relocations, malnutrition, and even torture. After escaping they may even have spent time in refugee camps with much uncertainty about their future.

Upon arriving in America immigrants and refugees alike often experience disappointment. Their knowledge of this country may have been based on movies or television sitcoms, and the real thing usually doesn't compare very favorably. For most immigrants there is a change in social and economic status when they reach this country. With a language barrier they are often forced to take low-paying jobs and live in communities that are unlike their hometowns. Role reversals take place within the family. The children who adapt more quickly become the interpreters for the parents, and are forced by circumstances to spend unlimited time helping the parents through mazes of paperwork and new experiences in order to get started here. Many immigrants voiced the feeling that they could deal with all these hardships and work their way through the relocation, but felt that the discrimination they endured made these troubles seem ten times worse and often led to total discouragement.

Adding to these concerns are the problems of overcrowding in housing; transportation that may or may not be available to get them to jobs; and the complexities of our social service systems. All the interviewees agreed that they felt compelled to learn the ropes and make it in this country. They felt they had to succeed here as none were willing to go home in defeat—and several had no home to which they could return.

These immigrants and their families have become assimilated into the American society, as have immigrants for hundreds of years. However, assimilation is becoming harder and it doesn't happen by itself. In large cities, suburbs, or rural areas, newcomers to the United States need education and basic social services to help them become the contributing members of society that they wish to be

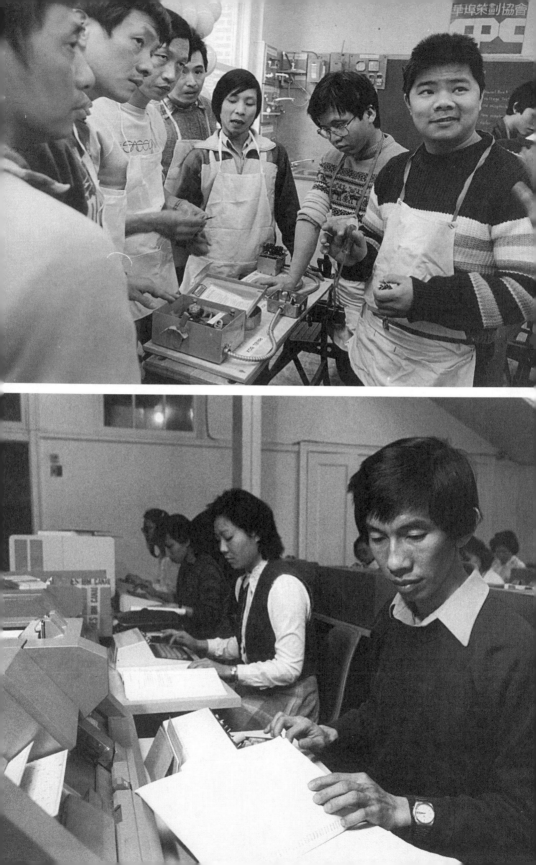

the contributing members of society that they wish to be and came here to be.

Earlier immigrants to this country often did not attend public school but went instead to night school. Today's immigrants, however, are causing profound changes in the American schools. Within thirty or thirty-five years it is expected that minorities will make up 70 percent of the student body in U.S. public schools. The education system and its professionals are scurrying to accommodate this influx. Teachers of English as a Second Language or Limited English Proficiency are often overwhelmed by students speaking ten or more languages in one classroom. In earlier immigrant waves we could rely on community and religious organizations to help educate the newcomers. But in the past twenty or thirty years this task has fallen more and more to the public schools, and teachers are often given little training to help them with the responsibility.

Our society benefits from this diversity and educating this growing population needs to be the concern of the nation, not just the states with the largest influx of immigrants. We need to see that these immigrants are getting jobs, and we need to help educate their children along the way. We need more teachers with minority backgrounds to better reflect the changes in our schools and society. More minority teachers and bilingual teachers need to be trained every year to help us make our schools safe and effective places for learning, to reach every student in our public school system.

*Top: A community group in New York helps Chinese and Vietnamese immigrants prepare for jobs in an electrician's training class.*
*Bottom: In another community program, immigrants learn office skills.*

*Arab immigrants in Detroit, Michigan, study English. The teacher is also a recent immigrant from the Middle East.*

The 1982 U.S. Supreme Court decision in the case of *Plyer v. Doe* mandated that immigrants, even illegal ones, be given access to public education. The immigrants in this chapter recall what it was like to attend some schools in this country. Many of their experiences were good, however, many others were not.

# THE IMMIGRANTS REMEMBER

— How soon did you go to school in America and what was it like for you?

— Do you feel you have faced prejudice as an immigrant in the United States?

— What has been your greatest problem since coming to the United States?

## Yetta

I worked in the grocery store with my brother Izzie till I met my husband. I worked in the store six years. I learned English in the store, by just listening to people. Then I learned the alphabet on my own and read a couple of books. I didn't have time to go to school. My brother thought school was only for bad girls, but I don't like to speak poorly of the dead. (Yetta's brother had died by the time of this interview.)

In 1918, I met my husband. A cousin introduced us. We kept company for a year because the war was on and he was expecting to go into the army. That's why we didn't get married sooner. The minute the war ended my boyfriend said "Yetta, let's set a date and we're going to get married." That was August 17, 1919. We spoke to each other in Yiddish or English, and he also spoke Polish. In the store when I didn't want anyone to know what we said, we spoke Polish.

Joe [Yetta's husband] opened a store in New York City in 1915, then he sold it a few years later and moved to Jersey City, New Jersey. That was the store he had when I married him. He didn't ask or tell me I had to work with him in the store, but I volunteered; that was my duty to help him because he was my husband. We worked in the store together for fifty-three and a half years. I don't remember exactly when we left the store, I think it was in the late 1960's. When my husband retired so did I.

## Miki

I studied English in Israel and I had an English teacher who was from England, so we learned British English. I could read, and when we came to the United States I was put into a high school program in New York. I started learning American English in my first classes, which were in math and history. Pronunciation was so different that it was hard in school. I felt lost. I came from a small high school and I had gone to school with the same kids from the day that I enrolled—eight years with the same kids. Here I was dropped into an American high school where they put me up a grade higher. That meant I went from class to class and to study halls, and I wasn't used to this. In Israel, we all stayed in the same class and the teachers changed.

In Rochester, New York, the kids at that time were carrying their books to class, they didn't use backpacks or bookbags. I said that's crazy, so I took my briefcase and I put my books in it. I didn't want to carry all my books but kept them in my briefcase. It was that way that I met other people who, like me, were very different. At that time, in Rochester, most kids tried to be very much the same, so I stood out. There was little clash, there were no blacks, there were no Hispanics. Everyone was white, not upper class by any means, maybe lower middle class, but that's what they were. Very clean and proper. There were rules about what you wear and what you don't wear, and how you behave and how you don't behave. I didn't learn the rules quickly and it was very different.

There were difficulties also because we had to pay for our own education past high school. We [my sisters and I] were able to do it because there were community colleges and there were loans. We were able to do everything we wanted, at every level—bachelor's degree, then a master's degree, and we probably could have continued on if we had wanted; education is an extremely important thing. It is so easily available in the United States, it makes it possible for people to reach their goals.

## Maureen

First of all, I looked a little strange. I had an odd haircut that was typical in Europe at that time. I had an accent. I had been a brilliant student in Ireland but I had problems in school here. Because I spoke English people assumed I didn't need help, but everything in school was difficult. A lot of things, for example, math and English, are very different over there and I was making mistakes in math and in chemistry because the British pounds and measurements are different. I was continually making mistakes but ashamed to ask for help. I just felt out of it.

The ironic thing was that another girl came to the high school in the same month as I did. She was from Germany and she was very popular and beautifully dressed. Everyone tried to help her and I just felt so shamed by comparison. I always thought why can't I measure up?

Maybe part of the difference was that she lived with her family and I was around a very spoiled cousin. It dawned on me that this was not like being with my family in Ireland who really cared about me. These people, my aunt and uncle, were unhappy with each other. My aunt doted on her son and so, naturally, my uncle resented him. My uncle was very fond of me but there were conflicts within the family that had nothing to do with me. Maybe the only reason they wanted me there was as a companion for their son and to be a housekeeper—like a servant, almost. My aunt started working soon after I came. I had to do all the housework.

Eventually I did make some really nice friends but what happened—and this is interesting—the less like an Irish girl I became, the more they liked me. For an example, some of us went for haircuts. Whoever did mine did a gorgeous job, my hair looked lovely. People became more friendly to me. From then on, I started wearing makeup and then I began baby-sitting so I was able to buy clothes. My high school counselor—she was an angel— every so often would call me in and say, "Maureen, see that bag? It's for you. Pick it up as you leave school. Don't take it now." It would be full of beautiful clothes. Between that and baby-sitting, I started dressing better and fitting in more.

**Chandler**
For about two months, we lived in a hotel. Then, once we moved out of the hotel and we knew where our permanent stay was going to be, I started school. Actually, I thought it was very nice. In school a lot of kids were very helpful. They helped me out the first couple of weeks. You know, when I came there I was pretty naive.

The first day I came in, the counselor introduced me to an Indian guy, so he could show me around the school. He did, and later on in most of the classes, the teachers tried to ask another student to work with me for a couple of days, to help me out with things. So yes, I had a pretty easy adjustment with school. I did not have any problems with it.

**Ann**
I think it was about a month before I started school, because we had to do some paperwork before we could get into the school. I was in the sixth grade then, it was fourteen years ago. There were not many Asian people in the school, just two or three.

At first, I remember it was just me—only me and one guy who was Asian—and the American people. Only two Orientals in the class and all the others American. I didn't speak English at all and when they said something I had to ask twice, "What do you say?" Sometimes they used sign language to tell me what they meant. Everybody was

*Through extracurricular activities—sports, clubs, or service organizations—immigrant students can sometimes find a place in the high school community.*

nice to me. But sometimes they picked on me, once in a while, because of the way I talk English. They picked on me and they bothered me. Every summer we had three months off, and the community had a special program for the students from low-income families. They were able to study and work, so you just worked and then went home. Many Asian people work there.

**Enrique**
I got here in June 1980, and I started school in September. I took a couple of classes in the morning, then

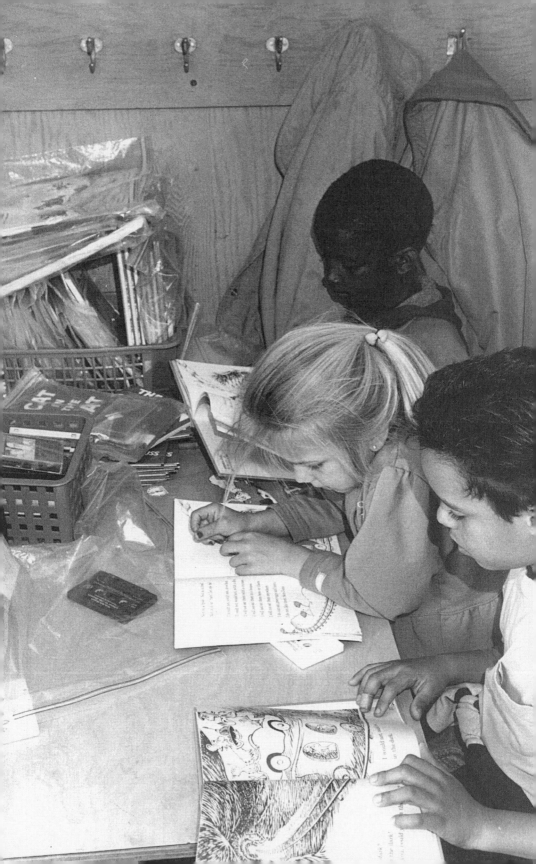

I would go to English classes. Some things were easy. There were some things we all had to learn and, you know, the only thing that was difficult was the language. Every week, there were new people arriving. People were coming every week. It was a poor school, with many Latinos. We would stick together, you know, and there were a lot of fights and lot of misunderstandings. Black people didn't know anything about us and we knew nothing about them. We thought the fun thing to do was to fight; we didn't realize how stupid it was. In general, for us I think it was harder than for kids now because the kids have gotten used to the pressures.

**Carlos**

I went to summer school when I got here because my mother wanted us to learn the language. It was annoying because it was very difficult, I guess. The people I went to school with would smoke and misbehave. But it was nice because the teachers seemed to want to be there and were great. I learned enough of the language to be able to go to school in the fall and to understand what was being said. In the fall it was terrible. I went to a regular school and there weren't that many immigrants. The teachers were not prepared to teach the few immigrant students. They were not sensitive at all. I used to get in trouble a lot because I did not understand what I was supposed to do—whether it was homework, or I didn't follow instructions, or I would arrive late to class—a lot of different things. It was just that I didn't understand what was expected of me. I think education is very important. Again, I think people don't realize how important.

My mother had already been here for several years,

*Young students learning English in a grade-school classroom* so she had a job and things were stable. I did not work when I came here, I just went to school.

**Nilou**
We came here in the summer. I spent a month in New York and a month here, and then I went to school. School went slow. It wasn't really any fun because I had to start from the beginning, I had to learn the ABCs and so I spent most of the time in English class. I was not treated well by the kids. I looked different and I didn't speak any English. I think that when you're ten years old or nine years old, everybody wants to be the same. At that age you have to fit in. Everybody dresses the same and talks the same and I just didn't. I wasn't accepted.

Some of the teachers were really nice, like the English teachers were really sweet, and one math teacher was really, really nice—Mr. Porter. But some teachers just didn't think I should be in the other classes. They thought I should be in the English class all the time. If I asked for my report card, they would say they didn't have mine done. They would say, when you get out of English classes then you get a report card.

There were twenty kids in this English program. I think it slowed me down. I tried very hard but fitting in didn't happen, and then I went to sleep-away camp where I was away from everybody and I had to learn to change by myself.

**Gabi**
I went to school in Lithuania up until we left, so when I came here I started seventh grade in December. I went to a private junior high school my first day and the teachers were very helpful at first, they helped me out with my English for a couple of months. My friends were mostly Russian kids. I didn't associate with Americans a whole lot. I didn't feel that they viewed me very well.

They never accepted me. I felt as though they were

looking down on me. I was pretty much by myself. I spent my first year and a half alone.

Now, I go to a public high school and it is better. I don't know if it is because by this time I am more Americanized—I look like them, I dress like them and act like them—or if it has to do with the fact that by now I've been here a few years and I feel like I'm one of them.

### Fassil

I went to school as soon as we got here. There weren't any language problems. In fact, the first year and a half or so I was exempt from taking finals in English because our grammar was better than the teacher's! Yes, yes, I was exempt from finals. I remember I slept through semester tests. I didn't have to take finals.

### Erika

I had to wait about a month because I had to have my papers ready. So I went to school two months after I came here. I started in eleventh grade. It was so difficult because I didn't know anybody. I didn't have friends. I used to study English in my country but I couldn't ask anything here in English. I couldn't understand anything because all the classes were in English. So I was in a special program to learn English. I was in level one. I guess I soon could speak English because I used to read a lot and have my dictionary with me always.

I was lucky because all my teachers tried to help me. Many people come to this country and don't want to work hard. Maybe they sensed that I was here to work hard. I was very different, and so the teachers tried to help me a lot, more maybe than the other people.

Sometimes kids who weren't Spanish were mean. At first, I didn't understand anything that they were saying, but they were laughing at me. That was hard because I didn't know what to say or do about it. You just have to live with it and get on with learning English.

Trying to work here isn't easy. First, you need to speak English. And then some people don't like you because you're Spanish. But there are many opportunities here and you have to try to take them. When I came here, I first worked cleaning offices. Within two years I was working in a dry cleaner. And now I'm working in Maryland with my parents. It's not bad because I am making money, I have my own car, and I am trying to save money for college. I think that it is very important for me.

**Anna**

I stayed out of school for a whole half-year's worth of classes. I came in the middle of the year and it was to be my senior year so, rather than attend half a year and then half a year the next school year, I just waited. School felt very different in Baltimore. I had many problems fitting in with students and with the work. I found the pace of life to be very fast, unlike my hometown. Most of the girls and the guys had jobs after school. Some had babies to take care of and their lives were so different from mine. The teaching style was so different, too. Lessons were slower and easier here. Things I had learned in tenth grade were being taught here in the twelfth grade and I was totally bored. My home school had been a Head Start school so we were very much ahead and used to learning well on our own.

Although I speak English as my first language and the majority of the students in the school are African-American, I was lost here. Students couldn't understand me and asked the most ridiculous and embarrassing questions. They wanted to know if we wore clothes in Africa, did we live in a house, why was my hair so strange? I dressed very differently from American girls. My hair was very plain and my clothes were too, but the other girls wore makeup and dressed like adults. I had been so sheltered and protected. I was not ready for this kind of life.

*In a community program in California, volunteers (often retirees) teach English to Latino immigrants.*

### Alice

I went to school immediately. I went into the seventh grade and I was upset about that. I had already started high school in the Caribbean, but when I came and was tested, even though I could do the work of ninth grade, they put me in the seventh. I was so upset, I wanted to go back home.

American kids discriminate. In the beginning it was because I was from a country they had never heard about, and even though I spoke English they did not understand me because of my accent. As a result I never spoke much. I just kept kind of quiet, to myself, but they would laugh and say, oh, you're from the coconut country. I didn't want to go to school and I cried because I wanted to go back home.

**Soo**

I went to school right away. We came in the summer and we went to school in the fall. It was another cultural adjustment.

School was really okay because I had learned English pretty well by that time and I was familiar with the alphabet and a lot of the words were similar. I had taken six months of English in South America, so I was a lot better prepared than I was when I went to South America. I was in a neighborhood where there were mostly Jewish, Italian, and British kids. In that part of Chicago, I'd say there were about two other Asians, Chinese who spoke pretty good English, so they were not totally shocked to see an Asian.

I made a few friends, but there are always going to be a few people who call you chinks. I didn't take it that seriously. I think afterward they realized what they had done. Not a big deal.

# FIVE

# Double-Trouble Teen Years

IN 1961, a young American-born boy from Oregon wrote to the president of the United States to voice his feelings about the immigration policy of the country. His letter was as follows:

> Sammy Smith
> Box 33
> Harbor, Ore.
>
> January 12, 1961

The President of the United States
The White House
Washington, D.C.

Dear Sir:

I am very concerned about the immigration laws. I think that more people may come to our country. I think it is our duty to make more people free. Not to be free is worse than being in a straight jacket. That is my opinion.

Truly yours,
Sammy Smith


Although Sammy Smith was younger than the teens interviewed for this book, his feelings were often reflected in the thoughts the teens expressed. These feelings sum up the frustrations of many teens because of their difficulty in getting to America. Once here, they then faced another type of frustrating situation in that they found themselves living in two different cultures, that of their family's homeland and that of the United States.

Each of the people who speak to you in this book had difficulty as a teenager in America. Being a newcomer has its own peculiar problems. Being a newcomer whose parents wish to keep you as old-country as possible while you strive to be as American as you can be, causes great hardships. We can understand why the parents act as they do, for parents always feel a need to protect their children and America can be frightening for newcomers of any age. Also, the parents are often overwhelmed by so many new responsibilities that the old-country culture and ways of raising a child seem to be the easiest and safest. These are the ways that have always worked; so the parents assume the old ways will work in America, too. The parents need to feel this security as they work toward residency status.

Today's immigrants to America strive for two levels of safety and status. First, they aim for permanent residence status. As a permanent resident, a person is required to pay taxes and serve in the United States military. During World War II, many immigrants proudly watched their sons and daughters join the armed forces to fight for the country that gave them freedom.

A permanent resident, or resident alien, is entitled to most of the benefits of United States citizenship, except:

*Community organizations offer classes to help immigrants prepare for citzenship exams.*

the right to vote, to seek federally elected offices, and to be able to hold most federal government jobs. A permanent resident also must wait several years before being able to bring a family member to the United States, whereas a citizen can do so almost immediately.

After five years, a permanent resident is eligible to apply for American citizenship. Although it is a relatively easy process, becoming a naturalized citizen can seem daunting. Immigrants hoping to become citizens must go through three steps. First, take the U.S. Immigration and Naturalization Service (INS) test. Testing locations are

*Young immigrants take the citizenship exam.*

provided throughout the country. Next, apply for naturalization; and finally, be interviewed.

The INS test is composed of twenty multiple choice questions on U.S. history or government. The immigrant is also asked to write simple sentences to prove an ability to understand English. The test takes about thirty minutes and is the only time such questions are asked. Classes to help immigrants are found through educational seminars. The naturalization application must be completed and filed through an INS office. Finally, an interview is held in which the interviewer can ask questions about the immigrant's application.

Once these steps are completed, the immigrant takes

an oath of allegiance to America and renounces past citizenships. Every naturalized citizen (meaning someone born elsewhere) is entitled to all the rights and privileges of native-born citizens, except being eligible to serve as president.

Many of the teen newcomers talked about how hard their family members were working toward citizenship. They seemed to understand that this goal often got in the way of family relationships as parents worked, sometimes at two jobs, and spent time at school or classes. Some teens were proud of their parents, others were resentful of this pressure on their family, and a few stated that they would never become citizens out of respect for their homeland. So many different feelings and extra work along with the pressures of maintaining two cultures made many of the teens feel as if they had double trouble and faced many more obstacles than most American-born teenagers.

## THE IMMIGRANTS REMEMBER

— How would you describe your relationship with your family once you came to America?
— Did you, as an immigrant teenager, feel that you faced a double burden of both a generation and culture gap?
— How did television help or hurt you when you came to America?

### Miki

Yes, when I was a teenager, I did feel a type of double burden. I was embarrassed to hear my parents speak their kind of English. In the beginning, it was such an adjustment. We did not have a car and in an American city in the 1950s you couldn't get around at all. There was so much trouble with transportation, but somehow my parents managed to go to work and we could walk to school, and my sister and I had to do the shopping.

We would go to the supermarket that was the closest, which was at least a ten-minute-long walk, and we would try to plan our shopping so that we wouldn't buy too much and we could carry it home. But at times these things were heavy, and they were in paper bags and we put them down in the snow; then the bags would get wet and groceries would fall out. It was hard to get all the food home.

It was exhausting, so when we got the first car, it was such an exciting day. It was exciting because my father was always crazy about cars and also it was a way to move around since otherwise we were stuck in the apartment where we lived.

I felt that my parents were so busy making ends meet, that they didn't have the same kind of interest other people tried to have in bringing up kids. They didn't have the time or the peace of mind to think about it.

### Chandler

No, especially in my case, I didn't change a whole lot. My parents are pretty easygoing, they really didn't push me either way; they were pretty flexible with me whichever way I wanted to go.

When you get home from school and you start watching a TV show, you learn pretty much everything. You pick up a lot of the language and culture—you pick up a lot of things from television.

### Ann

My parents were always strict with me and my sister and brother, even now she [Ann's mother] still is. She doesn't care whether you want to become Americanized or what, as long as you always listen to what she says. If she doesn't want you to do something, you cannot do it. You always have to follow her rules. It doesn't matter what you do outside the home, but you always have to listen to her, she is a very strict person.

We were not allowed to date. If she knew, she gave me a lecture. If she didn't know, that was fine. At home I always had to be very good, do what she wanted me to do. I could not become like an American girl and bring a guy home. If I did something wrong, I would be in trouble. I would be kicked out of my house forever.

## Enrique
Once I came here my relationship with my family was very different. We had been apart so we really didn't know each other anymore. I think the culture and the generation gap was not between parent and teenager, but that I held onto the old ways and my mother wanted me to become more like Americans. I sort of grew up with my grandmother in El Salvador so when I came here, there were some things that I couldn't do anymore, like hit my little brother if he misbehaved. Oh yes, my mother was really more Americanized than me!

That's really interesting, you know, watching TV; on weekends you clean the house, everyone together, my sister and my brother Larry. It was the whole family because I worked and my mother worked hard, so it was interesting. I had to do away with the traditional role of the man in my culture and work like American men do around the house.

## Carlos
Definitely [there was a cultural gap]. I think eventually our entire family fell apart. We were all so interested in our own things. Actually, with me it was kind of different in that I wanted my parents to be involved in my life.

## Nilou
Everything changed because my relationship with my parents changed. I was in such a bad mood when I came

home from school, and I was always crying; and my mother was just getting herself together and everyone was really busy with the new baby and busy finding jobs and standing on their own feet. They tried but I don't think they really gave a lot of attention to me. I had to struggle in my home in relation to school and it was okay, I don't hold a grudge or anything but. . . .

My brothers lived on their own; they were very independent and they could really get things done in their own way so I didn't go to them for help much.

The generation gap was maybe less than half of it. I think that 70 percent of it is the culture gap. They want me to stay away from the opposite sex. My mother wants me to wear certain clothing. I think I have American friends and Iranian friends who can really help me better than my parents can. I'm not considered Iranian, so there's a big culture gap in my home. It made it difficult for me and my parents for a long time.

I think on some things they try to compromise, say, to let me go out sometimes at night. Sometimes they try to be flexible but there are certain things that they are never going to accept. It's like beating my head against the wall; they are never going to change their minds about certain things.

I think they will have to trust me more because I think that I matured. I went to school, and I know what it is like to be in school and to be with American teenagers, and I think I know more about it than they [my parents] do. I think they know more about life, because they are older, but I think they have to trust me more. They have to give me credit. They raised me and so if they trust the way they raised me, then they have to trust *me*.

*Teenage newcomers are often eager
to adopt American styles.*

I think that there is so much more crime in America, there is so much more drugs here and parents have a lot of problems. They have problems here that you don't have anywhere else. Still, I would rather live in America; if it was between America and Iran, I would still rather live here and raise my children here, because the opportunities are still limited in Iran.

Everybody is faced with these double problems, because along with the generation gap there is a cultural difference. Other Iranians are going through the same things that I am. Everybody is somewhat miserable, or they try to rebel and they are miserable that way too. I think everybody suffers somewhat.

## Gabi

Yes, I think my relationship with my parents would have been pretty different if we were still in Lithuania. I think the major problem is between the teens and their parents. I don't think there is a cultural difference just because the teens are more Americanized, I think it's just because I am a teenager and they are my parents.

## Fassil

My relationship with my family once I came to America, how did or didn't it change? It didn't change at all. Some of the family is still back there, but most of us are here.

I think if I had not been almost out of my teens, it would have been different. With my kids it is difficult for us as parents to raise teens because of our values, the way we were raised. We want to instill that in them, but sometimes our ideas are different.

## Erika

When I came here I didn't care what I was wearing, what my hair was like, whatever. This made me different. I was just learning English and studying. I made friends and I started to dress differently. Mom didn't like it. She said that I didn't use to wear clothes like that, that I didn't use to wear baggy jeans. And now my clothes were all big, so my mom didn't like that. But I used to say, "please, Mom." I don't know—I just like it—what can you do? I dress the same as my friends. But she didn't like my friends either. I didn't use to go out, but then later on, I went out a lot. And she argued about that too. I don't want to be all day in the house just studying and working. I needed to have a place and a time to share with my friends. Well, I didn't try to become an Americanized teenager. I'm going to always be what I am. I am proud to be Spanish.

## Anna
I was nearly out of my teens when I came to America and I lived with an aunt, so I don't think I had generation-gap problems with the family like most other kids would. My main problems were with the people at school and life in the city of Baltimore.

## Alice
It did cause difficulties with my mother. Most adolescents have difficulty at that time. Oh yeah, more than ever, me and my mom we went through that, we could not get along because I became hostile, I was angry. Now that I am older I can look back and see that's why. I always had that attitude, I hated it.

She tried to keep me the way she would have if she raised me in my home country. She is still very strict. The other kids my age were allowed to go to the movies and be out at the park with friends. We couldn't do that because in the Islands they don't do that. You go home from school and that's it, you play in your yard and that's it. There is no theater. I mean there was a theater but only adults go to the theater. Children don't go to theaters, I don't care what kind of movie it is. So we never had that. Also in the culture where we were, women don't wear

pants. And so you just did not. Being cold here, we wanted to wear jeans and we could not, we had to wear tights with short skirts. People asked, "You always wear skirts, why?" I didn't want to, but mom was into that whole thing. Even after I went back home, after I moved out when I was eighteen, and I was going into town one day wearing jeans and she said, "You can't go like that." I said, "Why not? I am wearing pants into town, I'm not taking them off." So now it is a whole different thing.

## Soo

I did feel a double burden with both the generation gap and a culture gap. Oh, yeah, definitely.

When I was a teenager, my family was just getting established financially and they were trying to buy a house and having to put food on the table, pay for college, and so on. We stuck together and have to stick together. When I went to my college interviews, I was on my own. We could not afford an American translator. Had my parents helped out more it would have been good. I had to make the family phone calls, write the letters; if they had to, they could not.

Sometimes it was a burden. I knew if they could speak or write English, they would do it. They weren't lazy, they just couldn't do it, so I could understand why they had to rely on me so much then.

*A young Chinese immigrant in New York City's Chinatown will use her expanding English vocabulary to help her family manage life in a new, strange country.*

SIX

# Holding onto My Cultural Identity

FOR MANY new immigrants, getting started in America means amassing enough money to start a business or get married or go to school. Saving money is usually difficult for most native-born Americans, and for the immigrants it can be an enormous and daunting task, especially as they often work in low-paying jobs and have a hard time getting jobs in general. Fortunately, a tradition found in many cultures around the world allows people to participate in a money-pooling plan in which members share in a big payoff and at the same time enjoy the company of friends and other immigrants from their homelands.

This group-savings arrangement is found among many immigrant groups and thus is known by many different names. Ethiopians call it *ekub*, Bolivians use an Indian word that translates to "pass from hand to hand"—*pasanaqu*. Immigrants from Cambodia call this money-pooling *tong-tine*, and Koreans call the practice *keh*. Regardless of the name, members of these collection practices pay in a weekly or monthly amount, with the assurance that they will eventually collect the interest-free pot of money. Aside from the money winning, this money association offers its members a scheduled social time together as they meet for tea and talk of politics and hometowns.

Younger immigrants see these money-pooling associations as an opportunity to keep in touch with their roots and culture, to be reminded of a homeland they may never see again. Their parents are happy to see their children with other members of their ethnic heritage. Some immigrant newcomers see the association as a family practice that has been handed down for generations and that it is a practice worth preserving. The social bonding that results from these immigrant money-pooling associations is likely to be as important as the money saving aspect.

The immigrants who spoke about their money-pooling associations said that they take their membership and the responsibility of making the payments very seriously. "Reneging would be like social suicide" explained one Asian immigrant. Such a disaster can be as traumatic as the original move to America. Many of the interviewees said they knew their parents or other family members had participated in a money-pooling association. One person told of how the money had paid for her cousin's wedding and for a special dinner for all the group members.

Several of the people who tell their stories in this book said they might consider joining an association because it would force them to save, and by saving for the monthly association fee, they might spend less on consumer things they really don't need anyway. Since every member is guaranteed a fair turn to win the pot, the members feel perfectly comfortable that a money windfall will be theirs when their need might be the greatest.

Teaching a child to be thrifty and respectful of cultural traditions when the child is surrounded by America's

*Community houses that teach traditional
arts help newcomers retain their heritage.*

lavish consumption is another reason that immigrants
have given for belonging to a money-pooling group.
Nineteenth- and early twentieth-century immigrants to
America had similar self-help groups, but those associations have died out as the descendants of the original
members have become more assimilated and have spread
through the country. The immigrants of the later periods
expressed a hope that this weakening of the associations
would not occur within their groups. Today's immigrants
worry that people will lose touch with each other and that
contact with their culture could slowly evaporate as people scatter through the United States. Getting together at

members' homes or a neighborhood restaurant, they said, enables the immigrants to stay in contact and retain a sense of their homeland as they settle into a new land and learn its diverse culture.

As the immigrants achieve the American dream of a home, job, education, and leisure time, these associations help them financially. However, when asked the greatest value of money-pooling, each immigrant said that no price can be placed on the social atmosphere, emotional support, and friendship that comes with the association. These benefits are as bountiful as winning the pot in a monthly meeting.

Today women are beginning to take part in the associations on their own, carrying the membership for a single-parent family, or for themselves. Although at first this was a problem in some male-oriented cultures, more and more single women and single mothers are using the money-pooling associations as a resource for saving and for getting out to meet people. The associations can also offer male role models for the sons and daughters of the single parents.

It seems that these associations help many immigrants and have few if any problems. One immigrant told a story of a man and his wife who knew they were next in line to get the money pot and were anxiously waiting for the next meeting. They hoped to use the money for baby furniture and the baby was due in a few months. At the meeting, the man's friend asked if he could "win" for he had serious repairs to make to his home. These friends worked it out and the expecting parents were promised that their turn would come before the baby arrived.

---

### THE IMMIGRANTS REMEMBER
— How do you keep your culture alive today?
— How has living in the United States changed you?

## Yetta

Now I keep my culture alive by how I live. I visit my family. I have my grandchildren and my beautiful great-granddaughter who is gorgeous. If I don't see her for a few days, I miss her. When I was younger, I invited all the family to holidays at my house and we were all very close. We took care of each other and never forgot to help each other and remember hard times and good times together. I wish for my great-granddaughter to be a grown-up girl. I wish to see her start school. I wish it was twenty-five years back and I was a younger woman.

## Miki

Especially in the last few years, I have established contact with Czechoslovakia, and with the disappearance of the Iron Curtain, I have been able to go back and establish ties with my family there. Now I see that a person can be universal; I guess I think that way because I was born in one place and raised in several other places, and am now settled in the United States. I guess I probably do have some ties, nevertheless. I celebrate Thanksgiving and feel very American in the sense that I am involved in the politics and care about who is elected and why they are elected. On the other hand, well, I felt a great deal of happiness when the revolution took place in Czechoslovakia.

## Maureen

The Irish culture isn't super different from the American when it's all said and done. Of course, I have always loved Irish music and literature, and I have a tremendous number of books on Ireland. I like Irish music, but I love music so much in general that I listen to all types of music. But

I don't like the way the Irish culture was portrayed and still is to some extent.

Now, I am not Catholic, but you know, in Ireland on holidays, no matter what religion you are, you have the day off from school and people were religious all their lives. It's like Easter or Passover, on our religious holidays schools were always closed, but they are not anymore. In my childhood, people didn't wear green clothes—that was considered clownish, like going around in a red-white-and blue-striped suit. So you just don't wear bright things. Now [in America] on St. Patrick's day, people wear green clothes and are absolutely horrified that I am not wearing anything green. I say "Why?" They say it's St. Patrick's day, and I try to explain that people don't do that and nobody believes me. And then this thing about people serving and drinking green beer—I am just appalled. My aunt and uncle just laughed at it, and said it is kind of a distorted view of a national holiday, that it was no big thing—but, it's weird. It's so different and it's mindboggling the way it is portrayed.

## Chandler

We have a lot of friends from our country, you know. We get together every weekend, somebody usually throws a party. We have a lot of friends and they always have birthday parties with the kids, but for any special occasion they have a big party gathering, too.

How did living in the United States change me? I have changed myself not much at all. I am still the same. I don't think I have changed, same easygoing person, the culture is much the same. I would say I have more opportunities here to go into business.

## Ann

Because I work two jobs, I am so busy and by the time I get home, it is time for me to prepare to go to work again tomorrow. The only day I used to have off was Sunday.

We all live together, eight of us together. Because my mother is busy with grandchildren, it is my father who does the cooking. And, he cooks mostly Chinese.

Now that we are a little more settled, we have all kinds of activities, for example, New Year's, Christmas, any kind of holiday in my country. We always have a good time. People are very warm over there, we have a good time. Here everybody does their own celebration, they only do family. In my country, friends and family relatives come together and have a good time all day long. Here they do their own way, quiet.

## Enrique

I try to keep my culture alive because there is more of a need to practice it and to have people learn about us. Here you are competing with a lot of different races that are not necessarily your own, and there are a lot of people, many cultures all around. Yes, and cooking, traditional stuff and music, and language—you need all this.

Maybe I began feeling I was starting to fit into life here about five years ago. It took me ten years to adjust.

## Carlos

Food, and music, and my friends and I go to museums a lot; these help me keep my culture alive. I do a lot of reading, anything that has to do with my country, I try to do this so that I do not lose my heritage.

When did I begin to feel that I was fitting into American life? I think in my twenties. I am twenty-four now. As I got older I was happy to be on my own, knowing I had to do whatever I must to survive. I think I felt pressured by my friends my age who were Americans, and who were doing what they were supposed to be doing—like getting a job and going to school. I wasn't.

I think living in the United States has changed me. I think I have become really caught up in trying to get an education, to try to grow intellectually. I mean I think this

84

is really very good. Sometimes I think that a lot of the things that I used to value, such as family or sharing a meal, taking the time for eating together, I now resent because I feel I could be learning something, I feel that learning has become a priority above everything else.

## Nilou

Keeping a culture alive is hard. There aren't that many organizations in school for international groups, and I don't go to those. I really stay away from gatherings because I don't agree with a lot of their culture. I think I am partly Iranian, partly American—I don't know. We keep our culture alive by traditions and by the five holidays that we celebrate.

Yeah, I have changed definitely. In Iran, as a woman, I'd go to school, but universities are very hard to get into. In Iran I would have to get a job after high school and get married when I'm twenty or something. Most women don't work in very high positions, especially because the culture is very sexist. I'm happy to be here, the culture here is not sexist or is not sexist everywhere. Everybody is trying to be more politically correct here.

In schools there is a Spanish club, a Chinese club, but I don't know if there is an Iranian club. We are trying to make an Iranian club but I don't know if it will work, there are about eleven or twelve kids.

I think a club is a way of trying to keep the culture alive. In the Hispanic club, every Thursday, they get together and they dance, and on Tuesdays, they have meetings. I don't know what else they do, I know they dance Hispanic dances. We also have an international concert that we can go to and sing if you like, dance, bring food, you know, just whatever you want to do, whatever you want to present of your culture.

Some kids go to these clubs and dance and have fun, some kids think, well, why shouldn't we have a Caucasian club? The Irish, you know, they are getting out of it, say-

*Cultural or religious organizations, such as this
Russian choral group, provide a way for
immigrants to preserve traditions.*

ing, we should have our own club. Some kids get mad,
but its pretty much okay.

About fitting into American life, when I came to public school I saw that America is really a melting pot, it is
like borrowing things from other cultures—schools, building, furniture, everything from different cultures—and so,
there is no American way. You can't look at people and

say they look like Americans, because America is really borrowing from everything else and everybody is American and, that was when I realized I am American—because all Americans are different.

We should teach that people are people and everybody is the same, they just have different ways of handling their problems and different lifestyles, but we probably have the same goals.

I think that depending on what school you go to, it's getting more and more that way. We are studying African cultures and then Hispanic cultures. They teach us about other cultures more and more.

My friends are from all different parts of the world; my American friends are different, my Iranian friends are different, everybody is different, but the same too.

## Gabi

No I don't do anything special for my culture. My whole family is here, my parents. I guess we have picked up a lot of American culture, everything we do. Not that we think about it a lot, we just do it. Obviously, my mother makes Lithuanian breakfast at home and things like that.

I would have been totally different if I had not come here. It made me think about a lot of things. In my house I think I started looking at people differently because I have come into a totally different culture and I think I want to view people differently. I think I do view people differently. I still do a lot of things from my old culture, but as time goes by, I become more and more Americanized. I think I would have been a completely different person if I didn't come here. I am less sheltered and more worldly in my thinking.

## Fassil

Here, in the metropolitan area, there is a very large number of us. I would say approximately 30,000 to 40,000. And there are a lot of parties and things going on at different times, and also there are a lot of churches we can go to—I would say about fifteen or sixteen of them are around. So we are always in touch with the community. I have two children, a fifteen year old and a twelve year old. I am responsible to see they participate (in the community).

Living in the United States has changed me. You become exposed to a lot of things just by living here. You can learn a lot about life, a lot of things, but you pick up different customs and you are aware of other types of people.

### Erika

I never tried to forget where I came from or what I am, and at school it was very easy because I had many friends who would speak Spanish. All day I used to speak Spanish, the only time I would speak English was with the teachers when I had to work. That's why I speak very little English, because I don't practice. At school we used to have a Latino program. We used to dance for old people. We prepared a Spanish dance and went with a group to dance, it was easy to do that. But now that I am out of school, I don't have much time to go to church. We do celebrate our holidays but American holidays too.

Well, sometimes I think about going back home, but first I want to have a career. I don't want to go back there and just be nothing. And I study here and do something for myself. I plan to stay here and live my life here. I can have more opportunities here than in my country, in work, everything. More kinds of jobs, everything.

### Anna

My family and I still celebrate all my home holidays and all the American holidays too. We have family reunions and eat the basic cultural foods at home. This is very important. Because I was older when we left, I can always remember my country and the way of life. But my little

88

sisters were not as old and it is necessary to make sure they learn and keep a part of their heritage, really as much as possible, alive. My aunt has an African-style clothing store and my uncle is back home in Liberia so we get magazines from Liberia to help us keep in touch with styles and trends there. That helps with the clothing store too. I like all kinds of music and I listen to the music of my country too. I also keep my culture alive by joining clubs.

I think I started to feel more like I was fitting into the American way of life when I started college and got a job. I have worked in retail and in marketing, and met many people who were clients. I relate well to people now and am not so frightened! I spend a lot of time with friends from college and do not feel so different because there are many people from outside the country here in school.

**Alice**
I did not keep the culture alive at all when I was young. As a matter of fact, because I was taken away from it, I killed it. I didn't want to think about it once my mom said to me no, you're not going back. My grandmother was planning to move back to the Virgin Islands at that time, she was planning, so I told her I didn't mind going back with her because I just wanted to live in the Islands—it was closer to Nevis. My mother said no, you are not going. So we moved from New York to Connecticut and I was raised in New Haven. There are a lot of Caribbean people there but they are much older. They migrated years ago, went to school with the Americans. I had only American friends. I became fully Americanized. That's how my culture did not exist anymore. I lost it totally.

There were so many things I had never known, people would ask me where were you born? I knew nothing about the place I came from. I was a misfit and that was it. I would volunteer at cultural things because I wanted to find out more about them because I became very inter-

*Sikh immigrants participate in a traditional
service in a Sikh temple in California.*

ested in connecting again. So now I'm involved totally.
More Caribbean than American, I get into all the cultural activities and constantly promote my country, even
linking up with the other Caribbean countries. I'm very
very much into it. I am the only family link to the
Caribbean culture right now, the only link. The rest are
not involved at all, they are not even interested. I am the
only one who goes back home two and three times a year
and goes to other places. I will always go back to the

Caribbean; they won't and they are very much Americanized.

## Soo

Keeping my culture alive is easy. I work in a Korean church with a pastor and with many English-speaking Asians. It also includes Asian-Americans and people of other ethnic backgrounds. We are very exposed to Korean people at other churches, the largest church is about 3,000. We come into contact every week with other Asian people.

Even though we are English speakers, it's not strange for us to speak Korean. My wife and I speak Korean very well, we try to show the children Korean designs to help them to do alphabets and grammar. We will take them back to Korea if we can afford it, take the family for a vacation back to Korea.

I don't want my children to lose their Korean identity and their legal names. For instance, when they were born, I gave them English names, Nicholas and Nelson, but their middle names are the Korean name. I want to leave that in their minds and in their lives, even on their documents, that their identity is Korean—not to say that I don't want them to be fully American. They will be, but I know that when they grow up they will one day go to work and just like I was asked, they'll be asked what they are. It's Italian-American, British-American, Polish-American, and so on.

# SEVEN

# I'll Always Be a Foreigner

THE SMELLS and textures of a homeland grow dim over the years. Once-loved places become remote in a person's memory, yet the new place still doesn't feel completely familiar. Immigrants often suffer a feeling of not really belonging, of not having a home or country to belong to. Yet despite the fact that many immigrants in the interviews spoke of this ache, this feeling of being a foreigner, more immigrants keep coming to America.

Political speakers have been discussing immigration policy and issues frequently, and newspapers now publish more articles about it than most people can read, but, has there really been a change in immigration since the 1960s? Many authors and news columnists would like us to believe that the change is dramatic because such a belief would sell their books and articles. Those who support California's Proposition 187 would definitely like citizens to think there has been a big change. However, the truth is that in absolute numbers, current immigration is at approximately the same level as in the peak years of the early 1900s. The locations of settlement may have changed, but in relation to the total population, current immigration is actually considered at a low point. Our United States 1990 Census showed that 7.9 percent of our population was born in another country. This is not a staggering statistic yet we seem to fear immigration. The fear may be due to the numbers of illegal immigrants, yet even with those numbers the total is not alarming. In 1993, 80 percent of legal immigrants were from Latino, Asian, African and Caribbean countries. Immigrants of a hundred years ago were mainly European and Canadian. Today's legal and illegal immigrants are settling mainly in New York City, Los Angeles, Chicago, Miami, and Houston. The cumulative population explosions and social services drain has created a definite uneasiness over immigration. In fact, immigration specialists predict that 8 million newcomers will enter the United States between 1990 and the year 2000, making it a decade to compare with that of 1900–1910.

But, are the new immigrants different-looking from those of the past? Perhaps that is why some Americans perceive a problem. It is true that most of today's immigrants are people of color coming from countries other than Europe. However, Americans of the early 1900s viewed the newer European immigrants of that period, the Italians, Jews, and Poles, as different-looking, too. These immigrants were also viewed as unable to be assimilated.

The children and grandchildren of those who came at the turn of the century no longer feel "foreign." It is not even a thought in their minds. Although the people interviewed for this book often did refer to themselves as feeling like foreigners, they added that they hoped their children would consider themselves Americans. So are today's immigrants really so different?

Perhaps the biggest and most noticeable difference

*Arriving in the United States—the "Promised Land"
of many immigrants' dreams.*

lies in the speed with which these new immigrant groups
learn the system. They are not learning just the welfare
and health care systems; they are quickly learning the
strength of their numbers and the political power of their
voices. Ethnic groups are joining together to elect representatives who are from their culture and willing to fight
for the needs of their people. Working as a cohesive unit
will help people of color to better share in the social services available in each community. The biggest problem
seems to lie with the illegal immigrants who are taking
services away from those who are here legally and con-

tributing to their new country. Estimates vary but experts say that illegal immigration is as high as 300,000 people a year. This creates a sense of loss of control of the situation. These immigrants also represent a threat to jobs for Americans and legal immigrants. Concerns like these are being addressed by the National Commission on Immigration Reform.

Being a hyphenated American isn't so bad. Maybe the melting pot or tossed salad euphemisms or the concept of a multicultural country still hold true. It is a pity that we seem to need to learn this over and over again with almost each generation, but at least we seem to be learning it faster each time.

Is it true then, that America is still the welcoming "Mother of Exiles" as the poem on the Statute of Liberty claims? Or is it true that as a nation we have grown to fear the numbers of people arriving here seeking freedom? Perhaps we fear the number of illegal immigrants and perhaps we are concerned about our inability to secure our borders. Even with all these questions and fears, the poem that was written by a young woman, Emma Lazarus, is still appropriate. America still invites the "homeless, tempest-tost to me, I lift my lamp beside the golden door!"

## THE IMMIGRANTS REMEMBER
— Why do you think people come to America?
— What do most Americans know about your country?
— What would you tell newcomers to the United States that might help them in getting started?

### Miki
To look for a better future for their children, more than for themselves. Everything is relative, some of the immi-

grants come from very backwards countries, and even if they do only minimal jobs and get minimum pay here, they are much better off than they would have been in the countries of their origin.

I think the role of television is unbelievable, I remember coming home from school and watching the Mickey Mouse Club. I wouldn't miss it for anything and I think that played a very important part in my process of my becoming an American. Mickey Mouse is part of American Culture.

I think it is very difficult to say what Americans today think of Israel because there are so many different Americans. I think there was much more of a consensus in the fifties and if people disagreed, they were in trouble. But I do think there are many people who admire Israel and it's achievements as a young country.

My advice to newcomers? Take advantage of all the school available in the United States, since you need more education. And be sure to study the language first of all. I think it is the most important tool to achieve what you want here. Sometimes I think people come here and they don't realize how important it is to learn the language to be able to achieve what they want.

## Maureen

I think people immigrate almost exclusively for economic purposes. From some countries, it's for political freedom, but I think economic opportunities tend to outweigh other reasons for coming to America.

I think success here depends on where you are from. If you are from certain countries, people automatically assume that you are hardworking, honest, and trustworthy, but not if you are from others. At one time, it was a grab bag. Opportunities were there for any hard-working people.

I think, regardless of the problems I may have had, the fact that I was white and Irish and had good English

*Eager to earn a place in the American society,
young Latino immigrants work toward GED
diplomas at a neighborhood youth center.*

skills helped me a great deal and gave me a head start that someone equally intelligent or more intelligent might not have had, if he or she were a person of color.

Regardless of what jobs the immigrants manage to get, no matter how minimal, take advantage of any educational opportunities, and when I say take advantage, avail yourself. Night school or, if you are not working, go to day school, or even community programs that are not credited; and if you don't have good English skills, for heaven's sake, master the language because it's terribly important. People think you are nothing if you don't speak English.

Because Americans generally are not inclined to learn other languages, they are very chauvinistic about English. I think education is foremost, because living in America, if you don't have some kind of higher education, you'll have a terribly hard time. I think for businesspeople and real go-getters, education and the language are absolutely the things they need.

## Chandler

I guess it is the land of opportunities and if you want to be something you can be something. You can fill your goals a lot easier than back home you know. Back home you can determine you want it and you will achieve it but you will have a lot of difficulties. Here, it is very easy, you know, anything—school, work, or business.

## Enrique

I think it is possible for immigrants to come here to get a better life. But it's relative. I think that there are a lot of obstacles out there that are very unnecessary, and I think the obstacles have more to do with people's perception than with reality. That immigrant thing, I found that it is very confusing. I just don't know where the problem is coming from.

I don't know what Americans think about my country, but it is interesting how little public opinion there is; not many people know what is really going on.

I would only tell newcomers one thing. Come prepared.

## Carlos

I think that most immigrants come because they want a life for themselves. I think most families come because they have to feed their children and they don't have the resources to do it that well in their country. I think these goals have become harder and harder to achieve. A lot of people don't realize that to really survive, they end up working the whole time. They may end up worse off because they have to work and cannot see what they came for. I think the reason why a lot of people stay is that they feel they have to achieve what they came for. A lot of people never go back, they come here thinking they will make all this money and then they will go back, but that really never comes true for a lot of people. After a while it becomes the reality and they accept that.

A poor, colorful country is how most Americans perceive my country. I think people in general have a fairly good picture of Mexico. I am offended sometimes when people ask me where I am from after I have been with them for a time and I tell them I am from Mexico and they say "No way, your English is so good." Like I'm not supposed to know all the things that I know or speak all the languages I do, or do certain things that I can do, because I am from Mexico or from any Latin country or any developing country; that you are supposed to be inferior intellectually. It's really difficult.

After eleven years here, I still definitely think of myself as a foreigner. I could spend my whole lifetime here and I'm still going to feel like a stranger. When you called me, I was watching a movie on TV. All right, everyone in the movie is Caucasian. This kind of thing after awhile makes me feel there is no one in this movie I can relate to, there is no one like me. The next choice is a Spanish channel but that's hard too, because these programs have movies or shows from another country and I'm not there and the way they think is different.

I would tell a new immigrant today to be very careful what American customs to copy. Try to retain some of those feelings from the old country. Be really analytical and critical of anything that is presented, and think of the effects that it can have on your life later on. Stay really close to parents or friends from your old country, but at the same time try to in a way become Americanized, to get an education, and keep up. At the same time, don't forget that there is something else that is just as valuable— and that is your family and your spiritual life. And too, America definitely takes on some of the culture of the people who come here.

## Nilou

I think people come to the United States because there are more opportunities here. It's easier to get into a university up here, and you can get financial aid and all kinds of loans that are not given in a lot of other countries. Here people find opportunities for themselves because they care.

I think a lot of Americans don't know much about my native country. A lot do, but a lot don't, and some people are very ignorant about it.

The newcomers shouldn't worry about trying to fit in because when the time comes and they stay here long enough, everything is going to fall together—if they don't stress themselves out. Everything is going to fall into place and they are going to see that there is no typical American, that everybody is an American, there is a lot of diversity.

## Gabi

I guess immigrants come because they are either depressed or not happy in the country that they come from, or they want a better life, they want the social status, more opportunity. There are a lot of reasons why they

*Chinatown, Little Italy, Little Havana, Little Odessa, and other densely populated immigrant enclaves can be found in the heart of many American cities.*

100

come here. They do find more opportunities here than back in their own countries. I think it's harder and harder to get into college, even in America. For people my age it's hard to get into colleges and to pay for them and to get scholarships, I think.

When Americans ask me where I am from I say Lithuania, and they say "Russia?" They pretty much associate it with Russia. But for me that is really strange because I always saw Russia as a mixture of many different cultures and we never thought of ourselves as Russians. We were Lithuanians in Russia up until 1989. Most people automatically associate us with Russia and a lot of times I just give up explaining why it is different because they still think that it is Russia. They just view me as coming from Russia.

## Fassil

I would say that around the time that I came here, I believed immigration was more for education, but now I'd say it is more for economic reasons.

A lot of Americans are not familiar with my country. We never feel completely like we fit in America, we always feel we are foreigners. I don't know why, I really don't know why, but we are always foreigners first, that is how I think I feel. I am a citizen now and I consider myself Ethiopian-American. This is how I feel. Probably how most of the foreigners feel. It doesn't bother me at all.

I'd say to newcomers: start working, get yourself together, and then go back to school.

*The ports of entry—now often airports—still receive a constant flow of hopeful immigrants, eager to build new lives in the land of opportunity.*

**Erika**

People come to America because the economy in the countries—in my country—is so poor and people have to have more money for their families. Some of them come here because their countries are having civil wars. But so many people come here now that the opportunities are not too good.

**Anna**

Most Americans do not know the history of Africa, they think of the continent as one country and all alike. I must always explain it is a big land with great differences. Even my country alone has thirteen different languages. I use the example that people from Baltimore are different from people in Washington, D.C. and they are different from someone in Seattle.

I would tell immigrants practical things. The weather and food are so different from your homeland. Be prepared. I found the weather to be shocking because we have only two seasons back home, rainy and dry!

**Soo**

I think they come because America is a land of opportunity: educational opportunity, economic opportunity, a place where they can certainly be better off, if they work hard, than they were working at home. But sometimes, they are professionals—professors, medical doctors. They come with the dream and vision that they will be better off here. They come and then they realize that they have to run a dry cleaners, a Seven-Eleven, or a corner store instead of what they had hoped for. There is the language barrier and the difficulty of learning the language. It's just too much, and a lot of them are disappointed and they go back. I know figures show 35,000 people immigrated from Korea in the 1980s, at least 5,000 of them went back.

With young Americans and old Americans, I think the

perception of my country is different. For instance, my neighbor was in the navy and I think in the late forties and early fifties, he was in Korea during his service. He fought during the Korean war and all he remembers is little children begging for candy. That is the image many people have—of a ruined, destroyed, totally uprooted Korean people. Then those who have gone back now say, "Wow, these people have come a long way." Younger people, all they know about Korea is that its an up-and-coming Asian country that has recovered since 1988.

Newcomers here should know, just to get started, to be prepared to work long hours, be prepared to face discrimination.

# EIGHT

# A Food Potpourri

MY CONVERSATIONS with the immigrant Americans in this book all contained references to their favorite native foods. At some point in each interview, every person said that he or she still cooked some foods the "old way" and that these foods helped each one feel connected to the country of his or her birth. For this reason I thought a recipe from each country or geographic region would be a good way to finish this book. This is a spicy, hot, tasty, and filling chapter! Each recipe is either the favorite of the immigrant or one that represents the country. It will be easy for Americans to find the ingredients and prepare the dishes. Enjoy!

European Jews leaving the geographic regions of **Russia** and **Poland** brought many special recipes with them including this *noodle kugel* (pudding.) The ingredients are rich and fattening and were usually reserved for special occasions such as the New Year celebrations.

## NOODLE KUGEL
*Serves 6*

YOU WILL NEED

    1  *pound of broad noodles, cooked*
3–4  *apples, peeled, cored, and sliced*
    4  *eggs, separated*
    1  *cup of sugar*
    1  *teaspoon each of grated lemon and orange peel*
    1  *teaspoon of vanilla*
1/2  *cup of raisins*
1/2  *pound of margarine or butter*
1/4  *cup of orange juice*

DIRECTIONS

1. Cook and drain the noodles according to the package directions.
2. Use a little of the margarine (about one pat) to grease a casserole dish (at least 9 × 12 inches in size).
3. Take two tablespoons of the margarine and put it aside. Blend the rest of the margarine into the cooked and drained noodles.
4. Add all of the ingredients *except* the egg whites and orange juice. Mix well.
5. Beat the egg whites until stiff and then fold into the other ingredients.
6. Pour the mixture into a greased casserole dish and pour the orange juice over it.
7. Bake for one hour at 350°F.

The people of **Israel** have made the desert bloom with all types of wonderful vegetables. Most meals in this country include at least one dish, like this *eggplant salad,* made from vegetables.

## EGGPLANT SALAD
*Serves 6*

YOU WILL NEED
1 *large eggplant*
2 *or 3 hard boiled eggs, finely chopped*
2 *minced garlic cloves*
1/4 *cup each of minced parsley and onion*
3 *tablespoons of olive oil*
1/4 *cup mayonnaise*
1/2 *cup chopped pickles*
2 *tablespoons lemon juice*
*salt and pepper to taste*

FOR DECORATION
1/2 *cup thin strips of green pepper*
1 *sliced onion, 1 sliced tomato, and 1 lemon cut into wedges*

DIRECTIONS
1. Prick the eggplant with a fork, place it on a pan, and cook in a 400°F oven until it is charred on the outside and soft on the inside.
2. Let the eggplant cool. Peel off the skin and cut the eggplant into cubes. Drain the cubes in a colander.
3. Put the eggplant cubes in a blender and puree, or mash with a fork.
4. Stir in the other ingredients *except* those for decoration.
5. Place the mixture in an oiled mold and chill.
6. Unmold the salad onto a platter and decorate.
7. Serve with breads or toasts.

When the **Irish** were faced with a potato famine in the mid-1800s, they came to America in search of better lives. This *potato soup* recipe might have been made by one of those immigrants.

## POTATO SOUP
*6 to 10 servings*

**YOU WILL NEED**

> 5  *cups of chicken stock (canned is fine)*
> 2  *pounds of peeled and sliced potatoes*
> 2  *medium peeled and sliced onions*
> 6  *tablespoons of butter or margarine*
> 1/4  *cup chives*
> 1  *cup light cream*
> 2  *tablespoons all-purpose flour*
> *salt and pepper to taste*

**DIRECTIONS**

1. Using a 6- to 8-quart stockpot, cook the onions in 4 tablespoons of the butter. Do not let the onions turn brown.
2. Add the potatoes, stock, and chives. Cover and cook gently for one hour.
3. In a separate saucepan, melt the remaining butter and whisk in the flour. Let it bubble over a low flame for 2 minutes.
4. Add this mixture to the soup, stir to get out lumps.
5. Cook for 6-10 minutes more.
6. Use a blender to puree the soup.
7. Add the cream and reheat over a low flame—do not boil.

Most people think of curry dishes when they think of food from **India**. This *beef curry* is a little spicy and very delicious.

## BEEF CURRY
*5 to 6 servings*

YOU WILL NEED

2 *pounds of round steak cut into cubes (1-inch in size)*
*cooked rice for five to six servings*
2 1/2-3 *cups of beef stock or water*
2 *tablespoons of vinegar*
2 *tablespoons lemon juice*
1/2 *teaspoon of ground ginger*
1/2 *teaspoon red pepper*
1/2 *teaspoon dry mustard*
1 *teaspoon ground tumeric*
1/2 *teaspoon cumin*
1 *cup chopped onions*
2 *tablespoons butter*
1 *clove garlic, minced*
1 *tablespoon coriander*
*salt and pepper to taste*

DIRECTIONS

1. Cook onions, butter, and garlic in a big skillet. When the onions look clear or wilted, add the spices and vinegar. Stir briefly.
2. Add meat, cover and cook for about 10 minutes. Stir occasionally.
3. Add the stock or water. Continue cooking for 45 to 50 minutes. The meat should be tender.
4. Add lemon juice. Serve over hot rice.

A delicate **Vietnamese** soup made with asparagus and crab is called *sup mang cua.*

## SUP MANG CUA
*6 to 8 servings*

  1  *can of asparagus (white is best)*
  2  *minced shallots*
1/2  *pound of flaked crabmeat*
  1  *teaspoon oil*
  1  *minced clove of garlic*
  6  *cups of chicken stock*
  1  *tablespoon of cornstarch dissolved in 2 tablespoons warm water*
  1  *lightly beaten egg*
1/4  *cup chopped coriander leaves*
1/4  *cup onions*

**DIRECTIONS**
1. Drain the asparagus and reserve the liquid.
2. Cut the asparagus into 1 1/2 inch pieces.
3. Warm a medium soup pot slightly and pour in oil.
4. Add shallots, garlic, and crabmeat. Stir fry for 3-4 minutes.
5. Add chicken stock, asparagus liquid, and asparagus.
6. Reduce heat to low and let simmer for one minute.
7. Add dissolved cornstarch and stir mixture until it thickens.
8. Drop the egg into the soup while stirring.
9. Add a dash of pepper; remove from heat.

*Pastelitos de Picadillo* (meat filled turnovers) are a favorite in **El Salvador**. In this small but populous country, Spanish and Central American Indian influences are often found in the foods.

## PASTELITOS DE PICADILLO
*4 servings*

**YOU WILL NEED FOR THE DOUGH**
- 2 *cups of cornmeal*
- 1 *teaspoon salt*
- 2 *cups boiling water*

**YOU WILL NEED FOR THE FILLING**
- *1/2 cup drained, canned chickpeas*
- *1/2 cup each of cooked, chopped green beans, diced potatoes, and diced, lean, cooked pork*
- *salt and pepper to taste*
- *1 tablespoon chopped onion*
- *4 tablespoons tomato paste*
- *fat or oil for frying*

**DIRECTIONS FOR THE DOUGH**
1. Mix together cornmeal and salt.
2. Add the water and stir until dough becomes stiff.
3. Divide into 8 equal portions and let cool.
4. Flatten each portion until it is a thin cake approximately 5 inches in diameter. Use a little cool water if mixture is too sticky.

**DIRECTIONS FOR FILLING**
1. Mix all the ingredients together.
2. Place two tablespoons of filling on one side of each cake and spread it evenly on that side only.
3. Fold the other half of the cake over the filling half and press the edges together.
4. In a skillet, fry the cakes in shallow fat over low heat until each side looks golden brown.
   You could also make smaller turnovers for bite-size eating.

Most Americans are familiar with and fond of many **Mexican** dishes. This recipe for *plantain chips* is easy and very good for snacks.

## PLANTAIN CHIPS
*4 to 5 cups of chips*

YOU WILL NEED
    *vegetable oil (enough to fry all the chips)*
    *4 plantains*
    *1 tablespoon of chili powder*
    *1/2 teaspoon salt*

DIRECTIONS
1. Cut the plantains into 1/4 inch slices.
2. Heat 1 inch of oil over a medium flame to 350°F. Test to see if it is hot enough after thirty seconds by dropping a small piece of plantain into the oil. If it sizzles, the oil is ready.
3. Fry until golden brown in color, approximately 2 minutes.
4. Drain on a few stacked paper towels.
5. Put the chili powder and salt in a paper bag, add fried plantains and shake until chips are covered.

Another vegetable dish comes from **Iran**. It is meant to celebrate summer's delicious *herbs and tomatoes* in a salad.

## HERBS AND TOMATOES
*4 servings*

YOU WILL NEED

*3 or 4  large ripe tomatoes, sliced*
*1/4  cup each of cilantro leaves, parsley leaves, and mint leaves. Use fresh leaves if you can find them.*
*2  finely sliced onions, preferably green ones*
*2  tablespoons of tarragon leaves*
*1/3  cup of feta cheese*
*plain yogurt*

DIRECTIONS

1. Mix all ingredients except tomatoes, yogurt, and cheese.
2. Slice the tomatoes and arrange them on a large serving plate or tray.
3. Pour the mixed ingredients over the tomatoes.
4. Sprinkle the crumbled cheese over this.
5. Serve with yogurt on the side or on top.

Lithuanian foods are often confused with or thought to be the same as Russian food. There are many similarities but this *zagareliai*, little twigs, is from **Lithuania**.

## ZAGARELIAI

**YOU WILL NEED**
- 6 *tablespoons of sour cream*
- 3 *tablespoons of sugar*
- 3 *egg yolks*
- 3 *whole eggs*
- 1 *teaspoon of vanilla*
- 3 *or more tablespoons of flour*

**DIRECTIONS**
1. Cream the sugar, eggs, and egg yolks in a large bowl.
2. Add the vanilla and sour cream
3. Add enough sifted flour to make the dough stiff. Do this by adding a tablespoon at a time.
4. Pound the dough with a wooden pestle or mallet until air bubbles appear.
5. Roll the dough thin on a floured board.
6. Cut into strips that are 4 inches long and 1 inch wide.
7. Slit the center of each strip and twist one end through the slit.
8. Fry in deep, hot oil until golden brown.
9. Drain on paper towels.
10. Sprinkle with powdered sugar.

**Ethiopians** like eating *gomen kitfo* for the crunch of the greens with the smoothness of the cheese.

## GOMEN KITFO
*6 to 7 servings*

YOU WILL NEED

    1 *container of cottage cheese, 12 ounce size*
    4 *tablespoons of margarine*
    1 *garlic clove cut in half*
    1/8 *teaspoon each of ground cloves and cinnamon*
    1/2 *teaspoon ground cardamom*
    1/4 *teaspoon ground ginger*
  2 1/2 *tablespoons chopped onion*
    2 *teaspoons minced ginger*
    1 *green chili finely chopped, take out seeds—*
      *do not use them*
    2 *pounds fresh collard greens or spinach, coarsely*
      *chopped*
    *salt and pepper to taste*

DIRECTIONS

1. In a medium bowl, mix the cottage cheese, 2 tablespoons of the margarine, and all spices.
2. Let this stand 10 to 15 minutes.
3. Take out the garlic gloves.
4. In a deep pan or Dutch oven, cook the remaining ingredients in the rest of the margarine.
5. Serve the cottage cheese with the greens mixture on top.

The people of **Ecuador** export bananas and use a lot of fish and corn products in their foods. This recipe is for a *corn and tomato pudding* that is a little like a souffle but not quite as light.

## CORN AND TOMATO PUDDING
*4 servings*

YOU WILL NEED

2  *cups of corn kernels, scraped from the cob or frozen and thawed*
1  *cup of Monterey Jack or Munster cheese, cubed*
4  *tablespoons of butter or margarine, cubed*
6  *eggs*
3  *tomatoes, peeled, seeded, finely chopped, and drained*
3  *tablespoons of minced cilantro*
*salt and pepper*

DIRECTIONS

1. In a blender or food processor, puree the corn, cheese, and butter.
2. Add the eggs and salt and pepper and blend until smooth.
3. Stir in the tomatoes and cilantro and pour the whole mixture into a six-cup buttered casserole dish.
4. Bake at 350°F for 1 hour. Check to see if the top is browned and firmly set.

A regional west African favorite that you'll also enjoy is this *banana loaf cake* from **Liberia**.

## BANANA LOAF CAKE

**YOU WILL NEED**

- 6  *ripe bananas, mashed*
- 3  *eggs*
- 1/2  *cup butter or margarine*
- 1  *cup buttermilk*
- 3/4  *cup sugar*
- 4  *cups flour*
- 2  *teaspoons each of baking powder and baking soda*
- 2/3  *cup assorted dried fruit (raisins, dates) and chopped nuts*
- 1/2  *teaspoon salt*

**DIRECTIONS**

1. Sift together the flour and other dry ingredients.
2. Mix into this the bananas, buttermilk, dried fruit and butter.
3. Pour the cake mixture into a greased loaf pan (9- or 10-inch size).
4. Bake in a 350°F oven for 45 to 55 minutes.
5. Cool on a rack for 30 minutes.

**Caribbean** food often features seafood and can be quite fiery to the taste buds. This *shrimp with sauce* is definitely spicey and delicious! You can substitute lobster for the shrimp if you wish.

## SHRIMP WITH SAUCE
*5 servings*

### YOU WILL NEED
2 *pounds of raw shrimp, cleaned, peeled, and deveined*
1/2 *cup each of finely chopped onions and celery*
2 *tablespoons of oil*
3-4 *peeled and chopped tomatoes*
1 *bay leaf*
1 *teaspoon of sugar*
1 *tablespoon of finely chopped parsley*
4 *teaspoons of finely chopped jalapeno chilies*
   *(be sure to remove the seeds!)*
*salt and pepper to taste*
*grated Parmesan cheese*

### DIRECTIONS
1. In a large pan, saute the chilies, onions, and celery in oil until the onions are soft or almost transparent.
2. Add all the other ingredients except the shrimp and cheese.
3. Cook the mixture until thickened and most of the liquid is cooked out.
4. Reduce the heat and add the shrimp. Cover the pan and let it simmer for ten minutes.
5. Pour into a serving bowl and sprinkle the top with Parmesan cheese. Can be served with rice.

Americans often refer to **Korean** *bulkogi* as Korean barbecue. This is a dish that is typical of the country and can be made with chicken or beef that is thinly sliced and cooked very quickly over hot coals. You can do this on a barbecue grill or in the broiler of your oven.

## BULKOGI
*5 servings*

YOU WILL NEED

    2  *pounds of beef (sirloin or flank steak)*
    3  *tablespoons of beef stock*
    3  *chopped onions (green onions are best)*
    4  *garlic cloves, minced*
    1  *tablespoon sesame seeds*
    2  *tablespoons sesame oil*
 1/4  *cup of soy sauce*
 1/4  *cup granulated sugar*
 1/8  *teaspoon ground black pepper*

DIRECTIONS

1. Slice the steak from top to bottom along the grain. Make the slices very thin ($1/4 \times 1/4 \times 2$ inches)
2. Slowly brown the sesame seeds in a pan over a low flame. Grind the seeds in a blender or with a mortar.
3. Combine the sesame seeds and other ingredients in a bowl to make a marinade. Mix well.
4. Add the meat to the marinade and stir until coated.
5. Let the meat and marinade stand for at least 25 minutes or longer if you put it in the refrigerator.
6. Grill for about 40 to 50 seconds.

# NINE

# The Never-Ending Waves

AS IMMIGRATION restrictions and anti-immigrant sentiment build in some parts of the country, the newcomers to America continue to work toward becoming "Americans." Some newcomers say that they miss their old country, that there were stricter rules for raising children in the old country, that responsibilities were more communal and complain of the racism in this country. Yet, here is where they choose to be. The concept of America as a melting pot still exists and immigrants still work to find their way into the system.

In a recent USA Today/CNN/Gallup Poll, the immigrants surveyed revealed some very strong beliefs. Over 90 percent of the immigrants who responded said that they still believed in the American dream. As many as six out of ten believe that assimilation is the key to success in America, and most want to become (or have already become) citizens and vote!

Through the process of establishing themselves in this country, immigrants have changed both the face and

*One of the most famous of this century's immigrants, Albert Einstein, takes the United States oath of allegiance in 1940.*

heart of America. With every large wave of immigration this country has struggled with the problems of taking care of the newcomers, educating them, and absorbing them into the mainstream. But with each wave we have succeeded in growing stronger and passing on the ideals of this country. The newcomers come for economic opportunity and then adapt to the lifestyle of America.

122

America has always accepted immigrants and although there have been periods of limitations throughout our history, we have taken in people from all over the world. This openness has brought our country a wealth of energetic and talented people. The influx of immigrants in the last decade has frightened some Americans and even some immigrants too. Many critics of current policy say that immigration should depend on the promise of a job rather than on having a relative in the United States. Of the nearly 900,000 legal immigrants in 1993, 62 percent came here through a family relationship to a citizen or permanent resident; only 15 percent came through a job offer. Some political leaders, including both Senator Ted Kennedy and Speaker of the House Newt Gingrich, feel that the immigration system has been working pretty well and that more needs to be done to speed the assimilation of the newcomers. As you walk down the streets of any major United States city today, imagine how it would look without the multitude of stores, restaurants, and other businesses that are run and owned by the new immigrants. Our lives have become intertwined and we are stronger and richer for each wave of immigrants who have come to America.

# For Further Reading

Ashabranner, Brent. *Still a Nation of Immigrants*. New York: Cobblehill Books/Dutton, 1993.

Brown, Wesley and Amy Ling, ed. *Imagining America: Stories from the Promised Land*. New York: Persela Books, 1991.

Hoobler, Dorothy and Tom. *American Family Album*. New York: Oxford University Press, 1994–95.

Horton, James Oliver. *Free People of Color: Inside the African American Community*. Washington, DC: Smithsonian Press, 1993.

Jones, Maldwyn, Allen. *American Immigration*. Chicago: University of Chicago Press, 1992.

Koral, April. *An Album of the Great Wave of Immigration*. New York: Franklin Watts, 1992.

Leinward, Gerald. *American Immigration: Should the Open Door Be Closed?* New York: Franklin Watts, 1995.

O'Neill, Teresa, ed. *Immigration: Opposing Viewpoints*. California: Greenhaven Press, 1992.

Poey, Delia and Virgil Suarez, ed. *Iguana Dreams: New Latino Fiction*. New York: Harper Perennial, 1992.

Portes, Alejandro and Rueben G. Rumbaut. *Immigrant America: A Portrait*. Berkeley: University of California Press, 1990.

Rutledge, James Paul. *The Vietnamese Experience in America*. Bloomington: Indiana University Press, 1992.

Santoli, Al. *New Americans, An Oral History*. New York: Viking, 1988.

# Index